Jim Konstanty

MOST VALUABLE PLAYER SERIES

National League 1949
  JACKIE ROBINSON by Bill Roeder

American League 1949
  TED WILLIAMS by Arthur Sampson

National League 1950
  JIM KONSTANTY by Frank Yeutter

American League 1950
  PHIL RIZZUTO by Joe Trimble

MOST VALUABLE PLAYER SERIES

JIM KONSTANTY

by

FRANK YEUTTER

A. S. BARNES and COMPANY

New York

Foreword

OF THE twenty-five National Leaguers who preceded him in being chosen as the most valuable player in their league, it is doubtful if any was as little known previously as Casimir Jim Konstanty, the splendid relief pitcher of the Phillies who won the 1950 award of the Baseball Writers' Association.

Only Eddie Sawyer, the brilliant manager of the Whiz Kids, knew anything about the bespectacled giant who showed up at the Phillies' Florida camp in Clearwater in the spring of 1949. Konstanty had finished out the 1948 season with the Phils but had pitched only ten innings and was just another guy around.

Sawyer, however, knew Big Jim's worth from Toronto, where he had managed him. In 1949 Konstanty set the pattern of things to come when he performed brilliantly in relief roles. He was that *rara avis* of baseball—a pitcher who thrived on relief

▼

work. On the basis of that one season, Konstanty was reckoned as a factor for 1950, but nobody, not even Sawyer or his coaches, guessed how big a factor Jim was going to prove.

Not even Joe Page with his great relief pitching in 1947 and 1949 for the Yankees had such a season as Konstanty had in 1950. The big right-hander broke records and the backs of opposing batters with equal facility.

The story of Konstanty is an interesting one but a difficult one to write, since all of Jim's glory was wrapped up in a single season—although there is the promise of more to come. It is essentially the story of a man who perceived, an athlete who found the physical equipment with which he had been endowed somewhat limited, but who worked out ways and means of perfecting that equipment. The Phillies' first pennant in thirty-five years tells how well Jim succeeded.

Frank Yeutter, national president of the Baseball Writers' Association of America, has travelled with the Phils since the war, covered every game they have played during the Sawyer regime, whether at home or on the road. He knows what Konstanty meant to the Whiz Kids and he makes the worth of Big Jim plain in these pages.

Tom Meany

Contents

CONTENTS

Jim Konstanty

CHAPTER ONE

A Hero Comes to Town

FOR THIRTY-FIVE YEARS Philadelphia National League fans did everything but advertise for a winning ball club complete with built-in hero.

It was in the far-off, dead days—back in 1915— that the Phillies had won a pennant and presented to their loyal fans Grover Cleveland Alexander.

This breed called "Phillies fans" are a peculiar lot. In most instances they are older than the fans who root for the Athletics, the American League team in Philadelphia. And so far as the A's are concerned they just don't exist.

No fans in any city, except perhaps Brooklyn, ever yearned more for a hero. Detroit, in days of multiple pennants, had Ty Cobb, the star of them all; the Chicago Cubs delighted North Side fans with "Tinker to Evers to Chance"; Connie Mack came along with the $100,000 infield of McInnis, Collins, Baker, and

1

Barry; Washington had Walter Johnson; the New York Giants had Christy Mathewson and later Mel Ott and Carl Hubbell; Pittsburgh boasted of Hans Wagner and Fred Clarke, with Ralph Kiner for this generation; the New York Yankees possessed the incomparable Babe Ruth and Joe DiMaggio. Even the lowly St. Louis Browns had George Sisler.

All the Phillies had during those thirty-five years were a rickety ball park, a following of heartbroken fans, scrapbooks filled with satiric essays, a file of long overdue bills, and a perpetual lease on last place occupancy. Here and there during those thirty-five years, either a sparkling youngster or a still-competent castoff veteran raised the fans from their despondency—but not for long.

On the other hand, six blocks west of the Phillies' Baker Bowl, on Lehigh Avenue, in Connie Mack's Shibe Park there came a parade of heroes and winners that even now—more than twenty years later—are still household names among the baseball cognoscenti.

While Mack's star performers of the 1929–1930–1931 era were on view for all Philadelphia, they might as well have been in Shangri-La, so far as all Philadelphia fans were concerned. Phillies and Athletics fans never see eye to eye. To the Phillies fan Al Simmons, Mickey Cochrane, Jimmy Foxx, Bob

Grove, George Earnshaw, and Rube Walberg were interlopers.

Between Grover Cleveland Alexander and the days of Chuck Klein there was not a Philadelphia National League player worth mentioning. Although Klein went away to the Chicago Cubs and came back, he had lost his home run touch and his appeal to the crowd.

By the same token, after Alexander and through the days of Klein's great popularity, the National League team had fallen upon such drear fortune that total attendance for a season rarely went beyond 250,000.

The result was empty coffers and the establishment of a players' auction block. First one club president after another set up a flesh auction through which were sold players who came to rate with the finest in the league.

Alexander was the first to be sold along with his battery mate, Bill Killefer. Others who went the way of all Phillies flesh were Eppa Rixey, Dave Bancroft, Dolph Camilli, Pinkey Whitney, Klein, Lefty O'-Doul, Claude Passeau, Curt Davis, Jimmy Wilson, Dick Bartell, Spud Davis, Kirby Higbe, Bucky Walters, Moe Arnovich, and a raft of lesser lights.

Connie Mack followed the same selling policy, in

fact, he established the pattern which the Philadelphia National League club owners followed. The difference, however, was that with one or two exceptions —notably George Kell—Connie didn't sell his players until they had won pennants and World Championships for him.

He unloaded his bright, shining stars of the 1910– 1914 era, staggered along until the successes of 1929– 1931, then peddled another group of glittering athletes. During those winning years he rang up seven pennants and five World Championships.

The Phillies never let a really able player remain with the team long enough to become a favorite. Nor did they ever wait until they had enough competent players on hand to have a winning team. Phillies fans had to be satisfied with a vicarious pleasure in the deeds their might-have-been heroes achieved with other clubs.

Young players were delighted when they were picked up by Phillies scouts. Although they played for the last place teams most of the time, they lived in major league style and avoided a few unpleasant years in the minors. They knew that as soon as they developed sufficiently they'd be sold to the New York Giants, the Chicago Cubs, or one of the other teams that frequented the first division.

Then came the change in ownership that put the

fortunes of the Phillies in the hands of a man with a fortune. That young man is Robert R. M. Carpenter, Jr., scion of the fabulously rich duPont family, a Duke University alumnus and former football player, and a fan at heart.

Carpenter wanted a winner and didn't care how much it would cost to assemble. With the late Herb Pennock as general manager and Johnny Nee as veteran scout at the head of a far-flung scouting system, Carpenter's only orders were, "Get me the best ball players in the land. I'll pay for them."

Along came a raft of young players who cost anywhere from peanuts to the $65,000 bonus paid to Curt Simmons. As fillers-in came Jim Tabor, Frank McCormick, Schoolboy Rowe, Dutch Leonard, Roy Cullenbine, Eddie Miller, Emil Verban, Harry Walker, Hank Borowy, Rollie Hemsley, Bill Nicholson, and Ben Chapman—all purchased at fantastic prices from other major league clubs. Carpenter was out to win and win quickly.

The Phillies had moved out of antiquated Baker Bowl and become tenants of Connie Mack in Shibe Park. Phillies fans, dormant as Eskimos in January, came to life. As the Phils moved up in the league, these fans shook off their funeral shrouds and turned out in multiple thousands, raising the 1946 attendance to more than a million paid admissions, the first time in the history of Philadelphia baseball, either American or National League, that exalted figure was passed.

That was incentive enough for Carpenter to keep spending.

Still there was no genuine Phillies hero.

Rowe came pretty close when he won seventeen games. So did Leonard. Verban did a swell job at second base. Tabor and McCormick were occasionally exciting with their home runs. Harry Walker, winning the batting championship in 1947, was a minor gate attraction. Del Ennis, a local Philadelphia high school kid who was coming along rapidly as a slugger, had some following. Ben Chapman was a fiery manager. The fans liked him but never really got to know him.

Like his first boss in the majors, Joe McCarthy with the New York Yankees, Ben was a bench manager. Benny Bengough was the traffic director at third base. If anything went wrong it was Benny who took the slings and arrows of outraged fandom back of third base.

Actually the beginning of this successful era in Phillies baseball started on a hot July day in St. Louis in 1948. Carpenter called the baseball writers with the team into his suite, then almost knocked them off their feet by announcing that Chapman was finished as manager.

Chapman had lifted the team out of the cellar. He seemed to be headed farther up the ladder. To this day no definite reason has ever been given for Chapman's ousting. But that's a matter between Carpenter and Chapman and has no place in this narrative. It wasn't until the team returned to Philadelphia that the new manager was announced.

It was Edwin Milby Sawyer, honor graduate of Ithaca College, a professor of biology, a crack athlete who had had a chance of making good with the New York Yankees until he was injured, and a master at developing and directing ball players.

With all due respect to Chapman as a fine player, an indefatigable leader, and a daring tactician, there was nothing he could have done with the Phillies that Sawyer hasn't done equally as well.

Since there are only three newspapers in Philadelphia there were only three writers with the Phillies. The first was Stan Baumgartner, one-time pitcher for the Phillies—he was with the 1915 pennant winner—and Athletics and the only baseball writer in the country with personal experience as a major league ball player. During more than thirty years, Baumgartner learned a lot about baseball and how it should be played from the late Pat Moran and from Connie Mack.

Then there was Lanse McCurley, a competent reporter in every field of newspaper work, who ventured few opinions but wanted his "who, when, why, where, what, and how" answered forthrightly and intelligently.

And this writer.

It was hard to get to know Sawyer. Not that he was unfriendly. Just the opposite. He was urbane and agreeable. He volunteered little information but any sensible question—even after his team lost a close and important game—was answered willingly and completely. He never raised his voice, either to players or writers, and never turned loose invective even when a pointed question was asked. Some of his strategy was occasionally criticized. He admitted an error if there was an error; he defended his tactics and judgment when he thought or knew he was right. His door was always open, his welcome sincere.

During that last half of 1948 and through 1949 it became apparent that Sawyer was a superior baseball man—that he was fully aware of every move he made, that he possessed rare judgment of a player, that he realized to the last erg of energy the capability of every player, and that he possessed the ability to pass unerring appraisal on hundreds of players scattered throughout the Phillies farm system and on other minor league clubs not affiliated with the Phils.

Hence when Eddie gave an opinion the writers learned to believe in him implicitly.

It had reached a point where the Phillies were loaded down with bonus players, both on the parent club and on the farm teams. Some were promising, other were just so-so, but under the provisions of the bonus rule then in effect—it was repealed at the 1950 meeting in St. Petersburg, Florida—the minor league bonus players had to come to the parent club after one year's experience.

So it became almost a daily quiz, "How's so-and-so doing at Wilmington?" or "Will Joe Blow at Terre Haute make it next year?" or "What are you going to do with Willie Blank at Utica?"

Then, too, with the parent club were Robin Roberts, Curt Simmons, Charlie Bicknell (later waived to the Boston Braves), Stan Hollmig, and Jackie Mayo —all bonus babies. Any player who hadn't received a five-figure bonus didn't seem to figure in future plans.

At the end of the 1948 season when players from the Phillies triple-A farm at Toronto in the International League were recalled, the name of Jim Konstanty was added to the roster. It was worth just five lines in the baseball news that day. All Jim knew about bonuses and big money was, as Will Rogers used to say, what he had read in the newspapers. Certainly he had never got any of it.

No one had ever heard of James Konstanty around the Phillies.

"What are you gonna do with a guy thirty-one years old?" Sawyer was asked. "He's old enough to be the father of most of these kids you got around."

"I'm going to pitch him. What do you think I'd do with him?" Eddie replied.

"He's got a great record in the minors," was the sneering rejoinder.

"What's the matter with it?" defended Sawyer. "He won 13 and lost 13 in 1947 and he's 10 and 10 this year. Now look where Toronto finished."

The Leafs were a chronic second division outfit with one foot trailing in last place most of the time.

"Let me tell you something about Konstanty," Sawyer went on. "I managed him when I had the Toronto club. He's a strange character. He throws a lot of crazy, breaking stuff and he knows how to pitch and how he wants to pitch. I may start him here and there but we need a relief pitcher who can hold a one- or two-run lead for a couple of innings. That's going to be his job. Just watch him."

"How does he feel about being a relief pitcher?"

"We'll find out next year"—meaning 1949.

During the last three weeks of the 1948 season Konstanty was in six major league games, pitched ten innings and ended with a record of one triumph and no losses. Not enough to make any impression nor afford the basis for an opinion.

The year 1949 should have been a tip-off on what Sawyer had in mind and what Konstanty could do. None, except Sawyer, realized it.

In his first full year in the majors, Jim worked in 53 games, pitched 97 innings, won 9 games and lost 5, fanned 43 batters, walked 29 and finished with an earned run average of 3.25.

Then came 1950, the year that Konstanty became the first Phillies hero since Grover Cleveland Alexander.

He set the record of pitching in seventy-four games.

He was a surprise starter in the first game of the World Series.

And topped it all off by being selected Most Valuable Player of the Year in the National League.

Benny Bengough, Phillies coach who caught Herb Pennock, Dutch Ruether, Wilcy Moore, Waite Hoyt, George Pipgras, and Bob Shawkey and Cy Perkins, another Phil coach who in his days with the Athletics worked behind the plate for Grove, Earnshaw, and Walberg—two of the best qualified observers in the majors—agreed that in 1950 Konstanty was the best relief pitcher who ever lived.

Fanning one day in a Pullman car headed west, Bengough said, and Perkins agreed with him, "I batted against Firpo Marberry. I caught Wilcy Moore. I've seen Ted Wilks and Ace Adams. I saw Johnny Murphy at his best. None of them compared with Konstanty. That guy has ice water in his veins when he goes out there."

Praise of that sort from mates isn't unusual. That's the way most players are about fellows on their own club.

But then listen to Ralph Kiner, Stan Musial, Phil Cavarretta, Enos Slaughter, Jackie Robinson, Bobby Thomson, Bob Elliott, Sid Gordon, Walker Cooper, or Johnny Wyrostek. Summed up their opinions of Konstanty amount to "he's sheer poison."

Konstanty isn't merely good. He's great.

Had it not been for Chapman being fired and Sawyer becoming the Phillies manager, Konstanty might still be a starting pitcher in the minors. Instead he is an indelible line in the record book, an entry that may never be expunged, for pitching in seventy-four games in one year is a herculean achievement.

Now what manner of person is this Philadelphia hero?

He is not of Greek descent as a violent fan in Philadelphia insisted in a letter to a newspaper. This descended son of Hellas wrote, "There have been only a couple of Greek players in the majors. Why not tell the Greeks of this city that Konstanty is one of them. His correct name has to be something like Konstantinopoulos."

To which Jim replied, "I'm sorry to disappoint our Greek friend. My family came from Poland. My first name is Casimir but for the love of heaven don't publish that."

In appearance Jim doesn't suggest an athlete except for his 6 ft. 1 ½ in. and 190 pounds but he offsets that back of professorial glasses, his quiet, conservative dress, and his adherence to the hatless type. He's never very gabby but his early taciturnity has been overcome and he's a willing conversationalist. He never uses alcohol. He is an all year 'round athlete, an adherent to physical training and dieting, a devoted family man, and a precisionist at his job.

Each day he runs six laps at the ball park. After each game in which he appears he makes an entry in one of those well-known black books. He charts the number of innings he pitched, the number of hits he allowed, walks, strikeouts, runs, and earned runs.

He is an independent kind of fellow who likes to work whenever he's needed. His boundless energy and completely relaxed approach to the work at hand have been great for his relief role. The confidence which Manager Sawyer builds in his boys has drawn from Jim an admiration which has led him to assert, "We have the greatest manager in baseball today."

He is outspoken both in praise and criticism. When one of the younger, strong-arm pitchers chided him about not having a fast ball he replied, "Simmons has the most stuff of any pitcher in the league. Roberts is going to be one of the greats in pitching. My junk is pretty slow, but as long as it gets them out, I'll throw it up there. I do have a fast ball, I think. I don't want to be a starting pitcher. Let the younger fellows take the glory. I'll be content to be a relief pitcher and help them out of the tough spots."

On the other hand when he held out in 1950, a writer described him as "dickering" with Owner Carpenter. "I didn't like that word," Jim said. "It sounded as if I were begging for a couple of dollars."

Then, again, at a banquet he was told of the help he got from George Earnshaw, an occasional pitchers' coach with the Phillies in training camp. Earnshaw followed up his suggestion that the bull-pen mound be built up to the height of the regular mound. This made warm-up conditions an actual and precise aid to a pitcher entering the game. The first two or three pitches did not have to be wasted in finding the range of the plate via a home run ball clearing well-loaded bases, before the relief pitcher could settle down to the business of getting the opposition out.

The Philadelphia fans love Konstanty.

He's never too busy or too tired after a game to stop and talk to them or sign autographs. Success and adulation have not gone to his head. He loves every bit of it, as he has ten years of baseball drudgery and uncertainties to remember. But, according to the neighbors in his adopted home town of Worcester, New York, pop. 1,000, "Jim hasn't changed a bit from when he first came to town six years ago."

When a self-introduced alumnus of the University of Syracuse—Jim's alma mater—stopped him and asked if he remembered a guy who was in college about the same time, Jim pondered. He couldn't place the name.

"Oh! sure you must remember him," protested the intruder. "He was an ATO."

"That lets me out," retorted Jim, "when I was at Syracuse I was an IOU." (Jim worked his way through.)

After thirty-five years the Phillies had a pennant.

The fans had their hero. A guy they wanted to see. A guy they wanted to cheer, although each time he made an appearance the team was either on the verge of trouble or in trouble. He was their hero, nevertheless.

Big Jim Konstanty.

CHAPTER TWO

Strong Mind and Cunning Arm

YOU GET some idea of the eminence to which Konstanty has ascended as a Philadephia institution from an occurrence in the 1951 New Year's Day Mummers Parade.

Every New Year's Day for more than half a century the great, the near great, and the absurd have been honored or lampooned in this "merry, madcap mélange" as it has been described more fancifully than truthfully.

So when the miles-long 1951 pageant swung up Broad Street with an estimated more than one million persons lining the streets there were horrible caricatures of Stalin, solemn tributes to American soldiers, barbed lampoons on Secretary of State Dean Acheson and his "striped pants" boys, and burlesques of all kind at the expense of political and international frailties.

17

But marching alone, wearing the red and white candy-striped uniform of Philadelphia's pennant-winning Whiz Kids, was a character purporting to be "Konstant Jim Konstanty," Philadelphia's "Pennant Insurance."

Never had a Philadelphia baseball player—not even from great winning teams of the past—been so saluted in the pageant. In 1932 Connie Mack was revered in the parade. The preceding year in winning his third pennant in a row, Connie had been the recipient of the $10,000 Bok Prize, or Philadelphia Award as it is properly called, annually bestowed upon the Philadelphia citizen who has done most for the city during the year.

To attain such a tribute in Philadelphia's scheme of traditional things, where he is only a seven-months-a-year employee, Jim really had to be good and capture the fancy of the people as a whole—not only baseball fans.

During the seventy-seven games played at home in 1950, Jim became, to coin a phrase, the "toast of the town." In the tap rooms, in shop windows, on newspaper trucks—everywhere where pictures of the Phillies were displayed Konstanty's photo appeared.

Afternoon after afternoon, or—as baseball is gradually becoming—night after night, as Jim trudged in from the bull-pen to the mound his every step was loudly cheered by the throngs in Shibe Park.

Around television sets, the minute trouble seemed to be brewing for the Phils the first comment was, "Better get Konstanty in there."

Because of the location of the Phillies bull-pen in the extreme left field corner of Shibe Park, many fans sitting in the field boxes in that location cannot see who, or if, a relief pitcher is getting ready.

But it got so as the 1950 season progressed, that whenever one of the Whiz Kid fireballers was obviously weakening in the late innings and in a tight game, the fans took up the chant, "We want Konstanty."

Frequently when he didn't arrive at the moment they thought he should have been called upon they booed.

Even Jim, himself, recognized the moment he should be called upon. Often, without looking toward the bench for a signal to start warming up, he'd turn to his bull-pen battery mate, Ken Silvestri, and say, "Come on, there goes the whistle. Let's get to work."

There were times when Jim was so immediately needed that he had time to get in only a few practice pitches before he was en route to the pitcher's box.

When young, inexperienced pitchers, especially

fast ball specialists, fall upon evil ways, they frequently try to get the first pitch over the plate. Against batters like Duke Snider, Jack Robinson, Carl Furillo, Gil Hodges, Roy Campanella, and Pee Wee Reese of Brooklyn, or Stan Musial, Enos Slaughter, and Red Schoendienst of St. Louis, or Sid Gordon, Bob Elliott, Earl Torgeson, and Walker Cooper of the Braves, a pitcher who grooves that first pitch almost invariably runs into instantaneous trouble.

The Phillies couldn't afford to dissipate one- or two-run leads at any stage of the game, in either early innings or late. Although Del Ennis, Willie Jones, Andy Seminick, and Dick Sisler could knock the ball out of the park, the Phillies didn't present a consistently devastating attack as did the great New York Yankees teams, the Athletics of 1929, 1930, and 1931 or the Cleveland Indians of 1948.

The Phils were designed more along the lines of the 1939, 1940 Cincinnati teams managed by Bill McKechnie but were nowhere near as experienced as those excellent Redleg outfits. They had good pitching but Roberts and Simmons were mere children compared to Paul Derringer and Bucky Walters.

And so it went from day to day. Close games. Young pitchers weakening toward the end.

Ever-ready Jim had to be ever-ready always.

It wasn't only that Jim worked in seventy-four

games to set the all time record for relief pitchers. It was the regularity with which he had to be ready and to work. Playing a schedule of 154 games he worked in only three less than half the total. And was ready to pitch in at least twenty-five more but wasn't called upon.

In the early part of the season when the Phillies either won or lost complete games for Roberts, Simmons, Bob Miller, or Russ Meyer, Konstanty spent as many as eight days in the bull-pen without getting into the game. There were other days when the regulars were lambasted in early innings and he didn't even crank up, for there was no reason to expose his arm to the raw, penetrating cold of the East—especially Boston.

Once the Phils started rolling through June, July, and August, Jim was as constantly on tap as a keg of beer at a fireman's picnic.

He never complained. His calm manner and businesslike approach to his job in the bull-pen were at once a challenge to the younger so-called Whiz Kids and a reassurance to a rattled young pitcher, who had momentarily lost his control. He would never admit the possibility that he couldn't go in to pitch whenever Manager Sawyer called upon him. He directed his every thought and energy to the end that he should always be ready for work.

"It never was difficult for me to get warmed up," he said. "Even in the coldest weather I can be ready to go into the game after about twenty practice pitches in the bull-pen plus the few I take on the mound.

"My arm has always been limber and loose. I never had a sore arm or a pain or an ache in my life."

Jim has a degree in physical education from the University of Syracuse and studied physical education and coaching.

"I've learned to eat right," he tells you. "When I first started playing, I played ball to eat. I now eat to play the best ball I can. I eat a well-balanced dinner five hours preceding any game, with no hot dog or pop fill-ins. After the game I relax a while and by the time I arrive home I'm ready for a light lunch. Fruits, juices, and vegetable greens are now fun to eat because I have learned they give endurance to carry me comfortably through a strenuous game. A fellow should think, sleep, eat baseball. He should train properly, be observant, and help himself."

Jim is just as much an individualist in the way he pitches as in the way he takes care of his health, his appetite, and his muscles.

There was a game in St. Louis that meant a lot to the Phillies. It was a 3–2 game with Bob Miller leading in the eighth inning. A couple of breaks went against the youngster. He got one man out and the next two men reached base, advancing to second and third.

In came Konstanty.

The first batter he had to face was Stan Musial. As Miller plodded toward the bench, Manager Eddie Sawyer remained on the mound. Musial was bad enough, but the next man was Enos Slaughter. There was plenty for manager and relief pitcher to talk about. And pray about, too.

"What do you want to do with Musial?" Sawyer asked.

The problem was whether to walk Musial and set up the double play, which would have followed baseball's approved strategy, or pitch to him.

"I'll pitch to Musial," tersely replied Konstanty.

Later Sawyer said, "I let Jim use his own judgment. That's when he's at his best. He knows the batters who can hit him. He knows the fellows who will 'fish' for his breaking stuff. And most of all he knows when he's completely right."

As it turned out Konstanty was right. He ran the count to two balls and two strikes then got Musial on a pop fly to Eddie Waitkus.

Before pitching to Slaughter, Sawyer again went to the mound.

"What about 'Country'?" Sawyer challenged. "Can you handle him?"

Seeing that Bill Howerton followed Slaughter,

Konstanty hesitated a moment, then said, "I'll walk Slaughter."

Now there were two out so this strategy didn't figure. The tying run was on third base, the winning run on second, and Slaughter represented that all-important insurance run.

But Slaughter hits anything within the strike zone. He's a smart batter, cool enough at the plate to wait for the pitch he knows he can hit. He can hit to left field as well as to right and many times lashes a ball on a line over second.

Musial is the more dangerous, consistent hitter, but Slaughter is a mentally alert batter in the Paul Waner tradition who can hit the pitch he wants to the spot he wants it to go.

Konstanty knew these things. He knew his low pitch outside would invite Slaughter to hit to left field.

So again Sawyer let Konstanty have his way.

Slaughter was walked and the bases were filled. This suited Jim's book for he'd rather have three on, two out, Howerton at bat than have Slaughter slash a triple to left and ruin the ball game, although if he got the side out he couldn't become the winning pitcher. Just another game saved for another pitcher.

When Sawyer got back to the bench, his coach Benny Bengough, never a second guesser, took a sidelong glance at his boss as much as to ask, "If he can get Musial out for the second out, what's the idea of putting Slaughter on?"

Up came Howerton.

More than 30,000 Cardinal fans were roaring, for the Red Birds still had a chance for the pennant.

Jim's first pitch was a tantalizing, spinning slider, low and away for strike one.

The second pitch was in the same place. Howerton took it for strike two.

Here again was a situation that called for adherence to a certain operational axiom. When the count is two strikes and no balls, the pitcher must waste the next pitch—that is, throw it where it can't be hit or where, if the batter is impatient and nervous, he will swing and miss.

But Jim wasn't having any of the axiomatic stuff.

His third pitch was exactly in the same spot as the first two, low and away on the outside corner.

Howerton took it for strike three.

The Phils were out of the inning. The Cards didn't score although three of their best hitters—two of the best in the majors—had to be sidetracked. Jim sidetracked them and the Phils accounted the twenty-seventh of their thirty one-run victories.

It's a pitch called the "slider" that makes Jim so effective. Batters who have looked at terrific speed for eight innings are suddenly confronted by this darting pitch and their sense of timing is wrecked.

Now a slider is a pitch that many coaches, especially those training young pitchers, condemn and describe in terms of glowing profanity.

"Stay away from it," coaches advise youngsters. "Stay with your fast ball and curve. Learn control. Leave that trick stuff to the old timers. Forget the slider."

Just what is a slider?

As many times as that question is asked of pitchers, managers, coaches, and batters, that many varying definitions are proffered. It's everything from Christy Mathewson's famed old "fadeaway" to a combination of Frank Merriwell's double-shoot of fiction and an offshoot of the devil. Actually what it is, is a fast spinning pitch that slips off and down from its starting trajectory. But here's the catch to the slider. If it doesn't take that last split-second slide away from its course, it's a "setup" pitch for any batter. Even a pitcher can knock it "down town."

Many times when a close game is decided by a late inning home run, the slider pitcher, if he's the victim, will moan that the game-winning poke was off his slider that didn't "slide."

There was a night like that, that Jim still has in his craw. It was in July of 1949 in Shibe Park, Philadelphia. The Phils had a 4–3 lead over Brooklyn as the ninth inning started.

The Dodgers got men on second and third. Jackie Robinson was the batter. It was a situation exactly the same as the one that was to come up in St. Louis later.

Throughout their days in the International League when Jim was with Toronto and Jackie with Montreal, Konstanty more often than not mastered Robinson, although the great Negro second baseman was always a wonderful hitter.

But this night things turned out wrong. Jim decided to pitch to Robinson and Sawyer concurred, although the fans yelled for Robbie to be walked.

Up came Jim's third pitch. A change. But it didn't change.

Crash! sounded Robinson's bat and the ball soared away into the left field seats for a home run and a 5–4 Brooklyn victory.

Jim gave the stock answer. "My change didn't break."

When Sawyer was asked why he let Konstanty pitch to Robinson instead of walking the slugger to set up the double play, the manager replied, "I think that's the first hit Robinson ever got off Jim."

Konstanty went even further. "Not only did he never get a hit off me before, but I struck him out four times on the very same pitch."

The next night, Robinson, still gleeful over his home run said, "Jim's wrong about striking me out four times. It was six times up until last night. That one was revenge."

It was the same Robinson who made an amusing comment in the 1950 All Star game that the National League won 4–3 in fourteen innings from the American Leaguers in Comiskey Park, Chicago.

Konstanty was one of the four Phillies players selected for the National League team. It wasn't until the sixth inning that Jim got to work.

Robin Roberts pitched the first three innings and allowed one run on three hits. Dick Sisler had appeared as a pinch hitter and laced a single to right. Willie Jones played all fourteen innings.

But it was that sixth inning that delighted the National Leaguers who had been affronted by Konstanty during the regular season.

In that one inning Jim fanned Hoot Evers of Detroit and Jim Hegan of Cleveland. He had two strikes on Bobby Doerr, when the Boston Red Sox second baseman tapped an easy roller to Marty Marion and was thrown out at first.

It was when Evers missed the third strike that Robinson, playing second for the Nationals, yelled, "There it is! There it is!"

When Hegan missed three swings, again Robbie chirped, "There it is! There it is!"

Stan Musial, at first base, moved over and asked Robbie, "There's what?"

"I don't know what it is, but it's the pitch he always strikes me out on," replied Robinson, grinning.

Campanella, who caught Konstanty that afternoon, has also eaten humble pie fed by the slider ball ace.

"I caught that crazy thing," said Roy, later in the season, "and I swore I'd be able to hit it if he ever showed it to me in a game, but damned if I could.

"I dared him to throw it to me and he did, too, but all I did was either bounce it into the dirt or pop it up. And a lot of times I don't hit it at all. He calls it a slider. What I call it and him, too, ain't fit to print."

Actually the slider isn't Jim's only pitch. It's merely his chief stock in trade—his "Sunday pitch." He has a screw ball, a dandy curve, a baffling change of pace, and despite the occasional allegations against it, a fast ball of considerable merit.

Most of all he likes to pitch, wants to pitch, and wants to win every game on the schedule.

He's what Manager Frank Frisch of the Chicago Cubs calls "a great competitor," a general baseball classification under which are listed such modern stars as Eddie Stanky, Enos Slaughter, Gran Hamner, and Konstanty.

Frisch ought to know. He was one himself.

CHAPTER THREE

A Page from Horatio Alger

BACK OF this Cinderella Man's rise to fame and perhaps an imperishable line in baseball's record book—if not to fortune—lies one of the most fantastic stories ever to be a part of the extravagant saga of sport, where the unusual is never surprising.

Had Jim not met and married Mary Burlingame, a history teacher at the St. Regis Falls High School in upper New York State, he never would have met Andy Skinner, a Worcester, New York, undertaker whose hobby is bowling.

The famed slider never would have taken on that extra, required spin and very probably James would now be a physical education professor in some high school or college.

There were several long and fruitless years for Jim before he became as much a part of Philadelphia as Billy Penn's monument and as important an item in baseball's records as any player of any time.

There were years when Jim, who made a break on his own when he was but fourteen, learned the secrets of endurance and stamina; learned the need to use courage and optimism as an opiate for defeat and poverty; learned to make his own breaks.

Finally, through Mary and her family, he met the bowling undertaker and among them they evolved the combination that opened the door to success.

As a kid eight and nine years old it was evident that Jim could become an athlete. He was strong and a leader of the kids in his neighborhood. Jim had always loved every kind of sport and early spent all his spare time playing baseball or picking up balls for the local town teams, despite his dad's warnings that he'd never make any money picking up baseballs.

He was the second son of six children born of hard-working Polish parents, John and Apolonia Konstanty. Jim arrived on March 2, 1917, just about a month before the United States was drawn into the First World War. He gave his first wail to life in Strykersville, New York.

To Poppa John he was just another kid, another mouth to feed. John was born in what was Krakow, Poland, and knew few pleasures as a lad, certainly nothing about athletics which were indulgences of the aristocracy. But John knew about hard work from the day he was able to swing a hoe and chop weeds in the fields of the farmstead upon which he was born.

The Konstantys first set up housekeeping in Buffalo, New York, where John worked in the mills. But as their family grew, Apolonia looked to the country around Buffalo as the place for boys to grow up and work hard. They moved to Strykersville for a time. Shortly, they moved back to Buffalo where Jimmie had his first schooling.

The Konstanty boys ran with the neighborhood Ledger Street gang, but most of all, young Jim liked to play ball on a rubble-strewn lot "at the corner."

Jim was the first baseman, sometimes an outfielder, occasionally a pitcher. There weren't any "regulars" on the team. It was a matter of first come, first to get in the batting order. Jim was usually first on hand.

Still, Apolonia wanted the country for her boys and the family next moved to Delevan, New York, where they purchased a small country-town hotel, in the early 1920's.

This was a small rural town, but Jim found a baseball team here and then it was baseball—morning, noon, and night. Here Jim's father almost cut short a career that was to become glittering. Each night that Jim was late for dinner—that was usually seven nights a week—he heard the same admonition, "Get out and get a job and earn some money. You'll never make a dime at baseball. It's a waste of time." Nevertheless, Jim played baseball for the Delevan High team in 1931–1932.

But Jim's father came to know and like baseball. He became Jim's greatest fan from the minors to the majors and never tired of talking baseball to his friends. He lost his life in 1949 a few weeks before he was to make his first airplane trip to Pittsburgh to see Jim pitch against the Pirates.

A short time after the move to Delevan, Jim's mother died very suddenly. Apolonia had shouldered very capably the problems of managing her large and active family. Jimmie, only twelve, was grief-stricken at the unbelievable loss.

John now moved to a farm at Eagle, New York, near Arcade, where the boys went to school. Here Jim learned the rigors of farm work, and wondered if the hardest way of doing work was always the most profitable one. He missed his mother's good meals and warm loving care, but he filled up his time with basketball and baseball at Arcade High School.

When his dad and family gave up farming and moved to Buffalo where mill work promised a steady pay-check, Jim, along with his next younger brother, Johnnie, preferred to remain in Arcade to play basketball with what proved to be a championship team.

Jim's coach, Dave Collister, encouraged the boys to stay in town and gave them every chance to play ball.

Jim worked part time in Borden's milk factory, and the boys found a cheerless room to live in over one of the stores. Borden's paid Jim twenty-five cents an hour for the part-time work, but when vacation rolled around he was put on full time.

As Jim laughingly recalls, it took a lot of hours at twenty-five cents per hour to buy the canned soup, spaghetti, baked beans, and other belly-filling foods that comprised the daily diet of the two boys. Steaks and roasts were only names in the butcher's window.

But this was a case of stark necessity and survival. Both brothers pitched in with might and main. Jim started as morning fire tender at Borden's. During the summer, when he became a full-time worker, he received a dubious promotion, going to the shipping department where for forty cents an hour he packed and lifted 200-pound barrels of milk powder.

Here was a kid of seventeen tossing around burdens that many adults couldn't budge. To this day he remembers a big, burly roughneck twitting him about being a "young punk."

"Bet you a dollar you can't lift one barrel on top of the other," loudly defied the big guy as a crowd gathered.

Up came Jim's buck. Up went the barrel with ease. Another buck landed in the Konstanty brothers' exchequer.

Times were so rough, even with the increased pay, that Jim put in a 24-hour week end to get more dough. He went to work at midnight Friday, worked until 5:00 P.M. Saturday, returned to the milk works at 8:00 A.M. Sunday and didn't knock off until five o'clock in the evening. In all he put in twenty-six hours—each shift there was an hour off for lunch—and the net gain at the end of that session was $9.60 —a vitally important amount to be applied to room, food, clothes, and an occasional notebook.

But there was a rewarding recreation. From 1932 to 1935 Jim and John were the mainstay of Arcade's basketball and baseball teams. Strangely enough, he seemed to favor basketball at the time, and well he might, because he captained the 1933–34 quintet which won the B League championship before being defeated by Cuba, New York, in the intersectional play-offs. Jim pitched for the baseball team as well, and was presented with the most valuable player award at the end of the year.

Big Jim was really busy during his senior year. Besides throwing barrels around at Borden's, he captained three teams. He captained Arcade's first venture into 11-man football in the Wyoming County League, in which the team placed second. He led the basketball team which won the A League championship, only to forfeit the crown because of a technicality. He scored 167 points in fourteen games. Once again Jim pitched for the baseball team, of which he was also captain, and once again he was awarded the most valuable player award in athletics for the year. Small wonder, then, that enthusiastic followers composed the following song:

"Oh, it's Captain Jimmy a-comin' down the line,
  Well, don't that team looka hot, looka hot:
  As down the field they trot,
  If you listen you will hear
  Old Springville say, well I guess
  Old Arcade is going to win today."

Following his graduation from high school, Jim took up baseball with a vengeance. He played on the Arcade town team in the Suburban Baseball League, sponsored by the *Buffalo Evening News*, during the summer of 1934. He excelled, not at pitching, but at first base!

The team won the Southern Division title but lost out in the play-offs. The next year, however, it was a different story as the Arcade team roared through the regular season, captured the Western New York play-offs, and went on to win the New York State title.

It is small wonder then, that Arcade has never tired of remembering the days when Jim Konstanty played ball. The great ovation and welcome given to Jim at Arcade was a touching tribute to a young fellow with spirit and determination, who had made the most of his native talents and the opportunities presented to him, meager as they must have seemed most of the time.

Several of the town's able citizens, who had been responsible for giving Jim his first jobs, are now his greatest fans.

The help of the High School coach in securing a scholarship gave Jim the chance to go on to college —again to play ball.

After working the summer of 1935 to augment his bankroll, Jim arrived at the University with $160 in his pocket, half of his tuition paid, a first baseman's mitt in his suitcase, and the determination to graduate.

Before he could find quarters for himself—he couldn't afford men's dormitories and fraternities never entered his mind—he had to see about a job. All during his life until he became a successful ball player, his first quest wherever he went or whatever he planned had to be based on one thing—get a job.

The first job he landed in Syracuse was at the plant of Borden's, his old employers in Arcade. Only, in the Syracuse plant there's no powdered milk to handle. They make mince meat in that factory. Furthermore, there were no 200-pound barrels to wrestle. Mince meat containers weigh only 125 pounds.

There were more jobs to be had, closer to the campus. Jim became chief dishwasher at the girls' dormitory. Some students would pay extra to land that job. But before hiking over to the "pearl diving" parlors of the girls' dorm, Jim worked out a way to get his own meals by waiting on table in men's quarters.

A dandy day. From six in the morning until nine at night, leaving the balance of the day to attend classes, take part in athletics, and study. Yet the big, bespectacled fellow—he started wearing glasses when he was fifteen—fitted everything into place like a perfect mosaic.

He attended Syracuse University from 1935–1939 and became one of that institution's infrequent four-lettermen, winning letters in baseball, basketball, soccer, and boxing. He played third base in baseball until his senior year when he was switched to first, and was captain his last year. His coach didn't encourage him to pitch, especially as he preferred to play every day. He alternated at center or forward on the basketball team, and was a heavyweight boxer as well, losing to an Army man in the Intercollegiates his senior year.

Came graduation in 1939. That summer Jim tried out, unsuccessfully, for two teams. The managers of the Malone team in the Northern College League in New York State and Jake Pitler at Olean turned thumbs down.

But Pitler was to lament his decision in years to come. He watched Jim field grounders for half an hour in that summer of 1939 and told him he couldn't use him. Jake needed pitchers. Three years later when Jim was pitching for Syracuse in the International League and Pitler was still managing the Olean team in the Pony League, their paths crossed and Pitler demanded, "Why didn't you tell me you could pitch?"

That wasn't half the bitter pill Pitler was to swallow still later. In 1950 with the Phillies, Jim worked in twelve games against Brooklyn—won two for his own record, saved four for other pitchers, and lost one. The same Jake Pitler was coach for the Dodgers and had to take second place money as the Phillies beat out the Dodgers on the last day of the season.

Back in that fading summer of 1939 the moving

finger of fate was at work. Jim had his diploma from Syracuse and a job as a physical education teacher.

That autumn and winter he taught at the Endwell, New York, High School, returned to college for some graduate work, played professional basketball with Binghamton, fiddled around with more baseball in the spring of 1940, and finally accepted a job as "phys ed" teacher at the St. Regis Falls High School.

He was about ready to quit baseball. That's where Mary Burlingame enters the picture and introduces a chapter of fantasy in the athlete's life.

CHAPTER FOUR

Love and an Undertaker

MARY BURLINGAME had been teaching at St. Regis Falls High School for two years when Jim arrived to take the "phys ed" job and coach the athletic teams.

Mary was an intelligent young woman, interested in sports and the teaching job at St. Regis. She had spent her childhood growing up in the friendly, wholesome town of Worcester, New York, where her father, Menzo Burlingame, had been the high school principal and later superintendent of schools. After his death in 1922, when Mary was five years old, her mother, Elizabeth Burlingame, taught social studies in the school to support the family of four children.

Theirs was a safe and protected little world despite the rigors of making ends meet with four to feed and clothe and educate. Living in Worcester was a simple

43

affair for the kids growing up there. Swimming through the long lazy summers; skiing and skating and sleigh-riding in the crisp cold snowy winters; high-pitched excitement over local basketball rivalries; whooping it up for the local baseball teams; school dances and parties—all supplied a variety of entertainment for Mary through the high-school years.

Upon graduation from nearby Albany State Teachers College in 1938, Mary began to teach history at the St. Regis Falls Central School in northern New York, at one time a busy lumbering area.

A young teacher's life becomes filled with papers to mark, lessons to chart, dances to sponsor, new friendships with young people bursting with all sorts of growing pains and enthusiasms.

Mary was an attractive brunette, with brown hair and eyes, a trim figure, and a friendly, gracious manner. Her youthful, schoolgirl appearance was a matter of regret as a beginning teacher.

Mary was the first sight Jim's eyes dwelt upon as he attended his first faculty meeting in that September of 1940. The high school principal and the other members of the faculty were gathered in the conference room.

"Meet Mr. Konstanty," said the principal, then proceeded to identify each of the teachers around the table. The names were a jumble of words to Jim. He saw no one but Mary.

Here was a star athlete being presented. The academic teachers weren't slightly impressed. Not a male member of the faculty had ever won a varsity letter, not even freshman numerals, at their colleges. At Syracuse Jim was a "big man" on the campus.

What Jim saw, displayed in the usual false modesty, were brightly blinking Phi Beta Kappa keys, dangling from watch chains. Jim had been a Grade A student but here were language, history, mathematics, and logic teachers—a clannish lot whose most intimate knowledge of athletics recognized the difference between a touchdown and a foul ball.

Jim was as impressed as a bronze Buddha contemplating prayer papers. All he could see was Mary.

"I'm going to see a lot more of that gal," said Jim to himself.

Mary had other ideas at the time, also a beau. Here was a Grand National hurdle for Jim to take. She was so friendly, but so difficult to impress.

She fancied winter sports, occasionally. Autumn didn't mean football games to her. It meant long hikes in the country. Winter meant skiing and ice skating. She performed beautifully both on skis and skates. If Jim contemplated skis, about the only thought that came to his mind were the staves in the barrels he used to toss around in Borden's shipping room.

Time after time Jim tried to date Mary. Time after time he received polite refusals. But Mary didn't know Jim. When he made up his mind to accomplish something he succeeded. So about Thanksgiving— two months after that faculty meeting—Jim had his first date with Mary. From then on Mary might just as well have prepared to become Mrs. Konstanty one day.

When winter brought the soft, powdery snow to delight the skiing crowd, Mary and her group were in their element. Here was one place Jim couldn't bother her.

No?

Jim borrowed a pair of skis. He didn't even know how to put them on. A week or so later he not only knew how to put them on but when Mary's crowd went on a cross-country ski jaunt there was Jim joining in, getting along clumsily, but staying with the pack. On a downhill slalom he tumbled and almost killed himself. How he escaped without broken bones or a broken neck is still a mystery to Mary. Jim was graceful enough as a basketball and baseball player but skiing was not his métier.

When there was a school dance the story was different. Mary allowed Jim one or two courtesy dances on her program. He spent the rest of the evening "cutting in" on her partners. The scholarly male teachers were absorbing and entertaining in conversation, but on the dance floor Jim was the number one boy. He had the native grace and rhythm of a trained athlete.

Finally Mary quit resisting Jim's invitations. They began going places together. Dinner once in a while when Jim's bankroll was adequate. Or to the movies on nights when Mary didn't have test papers to mark. Sometimes just for walks. Jim never lost a chance of seeing her. They even ate their luncheon sandwiches together at the local restaurant.

It was on New Year's Eve of 1940. They went together to a dance. Jim proposed. Mary demurred from a direct acceptance.

Springtime came for Mary and Jim. Our hero was assigned to the Springfield team of the Eastern League. It meant getting a leave of absence from teaching and attending baseball training camp. He and Mary would be separated.

Once Jim departed, Mary knew the right answer. She'd marry the big guy. And so on May 27, 1941, when Jim came back, they were married.

There were a lot of baseball trials and failures

through this period but they belong in another chapter. This has to do with an outside phase that started in 1945. Those years weren't fruitful for Jim as a pitcher and in 1944 when it appeared that he was en route to military service, he and Mary moved to the Burlingame home in Worcester.

That's where Undertaker Andy Skinner enters the scheme of things.

Andy's family had lived in Worcester for more than sixty years. His father had built the undertaking business. After attending Hamilton College, Andy joined his father in the undertaking business, which was connected with a store down "in town" that was the gathering place for young and old.

The Skinner family lived diagonally across the street from the Burlingames. Everyone in town knew that Mary Burlingame was married to Jim Konstanty, the Syracuse athlete. So Andy made a social call, introduced himself to Jim, and invited him to the Skinner shooting cabin up in the woods. They became close friends. Jim became one of the regulars to stop in for a chat with Andy. They talked sports, war, and every other topic that is dwelt upon in small town, and even big city, informal meeting places.

Jim played pro basketball out of Utica. Andy often rode along to the games. The talk often got around to baseball, and a new pitch Jim was working on. He couldn't figure out why it broke sometimes, but often came up straight to the plate.

In the spring of 1946 Jim was holding out to the Toronto Maple Leafs. One night Skinner said, "While you're waiting to report to Florida why don't we take some baseball stuff over to the school gym and play catch?"

They took gloves and a ball that night.

Andy had never played anything but high school baseball. But he loved it. He put on the catcher's glove and Jim did the pitching. Occasionally a pitch took a crazy dip and eluded Andy. The next few tosses were right down the middle.

Skinner wondered why some pitches broke sharply and others didn't.

"I've been trying to figure that out for a long time," Jim admitted. "When I get that good break on the ball I win. When it's straight I get into trouble."

Skinner had a quick eye, a deliberate way of figuring on things. He remembered something about his bowling problems.

"You know, Jim," he mused, "if you'll put more spin on the ball it will break more. Any sphere will deviate from its course if it is spinning. The more spin the more deviation. How do you throw that darting pitch?"

Andy knew so little about baseball that he didn't

even call it a "curve" ball, which it wasn't, but which would be the natural term for a layman to use for any ball that didn't follow a straight line.

Jim showed how he let it come off the outside of his index finger, at the same time snapping his arm sharply downward.

"I think that you let it come off the tips of your fingers sometimes," Andy said. "That's what keeps it from breaking. You concentrate on spinning it from the outside each time and it's got to break."

Jim didn't have to worry about control. He always had that. During the All Star game in 1950, when he was warming up in the National League bull-pen with Coach Clyde Sukeforth of Brooklyn, his control was so unerring that the veteran catcher marveled. Of course, Jim had arrived by that time, but Sukeforth, who had caught some great pitchers in his twenty-four years in organized baseball, sincerely declared he had never seen a pitcher call for the number of targets Jim did, then hit them as if he had zeroed in with a telescopic sight.

The problem at this moment was application of spin. The Skinner Theory became an important part of Jim's daily thinking.

After service with the Navy and another start in the minors, without earth-shaking successes, Jim joined the Phillies at the end of the 1948 season.

Then came the great year of 1950.

Although there were many trying days of baseball between the beginning of the Skinner experiment and the 1950 rise to fame, they will be treated upon later. This part belongs to Mary and Andy.

It was July, 1950, hot as the blue blazes of Hades and Jim up to his neck in relief work. During the last day of June and the first two days of July, Jim worked in four games against Brooklyn. On the Fourth of July, in the second game of the holiday double-header, Jim experienced the worst humiliation of his career.

It was a free-hitting game between the Phillies and Boston Braves. The Braves led 7–0 as the second inning closed. The Phils made four runs. It was 7–4. The Phils got their fifth run in the third inning. The Braves made one in the sixth and the Phils collected a brace of runs in each of the sixth and seventh innings to go ahead 9–8.

Here came Konstanty to hold that one-run lead. He succeeded in the seventh and eighth innings but in the ninth the heavens collapsed on him.

Willard Marshall singled. Roy Hartsfield doubled. Sam Jethroe was purposely passed to fill the bases. There was one out. Bob Elliott made it two by missing three swings.

But with the count ball one, strike one, Sid Gordon

hit a grand slam home run into the upper left field seats. Four runs poured across the plate and the Braves won 12–9.

It was the bitterest dose Jim ever had to swallow.

That night, when he went home to the attractive house where he and Mary and the two children, Jim and Helen, lived in Ardmore on the Main Line, he was disconsolate.

"I've lost that darn slider again," he told Mary. "Doggone it! Gordon's got no right to hit that pitch the way he did."

"That's what he's supposed to do, isn't it?" reasoned Mary.

"Yes, but not when that pitch is right. I'm doing something wrong. I'm going to call Andy."

It was a matter of minutes before his undertaking pal in Worcester was on the other end of the line.

"Listen, Andy, I'm doing something wrong. Could you come down and straighten me out?" Jim pleaded.

"Are you spinning the ball right?" asked Andy.

"I don't know, I guess not."

"All right, I'll be down tomorrow. Take it easy. We'll get it worked out."

Next day, the smallish, sandy-haired, bespectacled undertaker, with the intent eyes and quiet manner arrived at Shibe Park.

Jim wasn't needed that afternoon, for Russ Meyer defeated the New York Giants 10–3.

After the game Philadelphia and New York writers were still tapping out their pieces in the press box, and a few hundred fans tarried to make the usual, curious inspection of a big league park. Jim, in uniform, and his little pal, in street clothes, went to the bull-pen.

Andy took off his coat and rolled up his sleeves. He didn't even bother to remove his glasses. Jim started to throw.

"What's Konstanty doing out there?" one after another of the writers asked. Some of the fans started out toward the bull-pen for their own investigation. They were shooed away.

Jim pitched maybe a dozen times. Skinner shook his head like a medical diagnostician mulling over a puzzling symptom.

"Jim, there's absolutely no spin on that pitch," Andy said. "A kid could hit it. No wonder Gordon banged it out of the park. Let's try again."

Another twenty pitches or so. Still no spin. It was a pitch, tailor-made for home run sluggers.

Andy threw aside the catcher's glove.

"Let's forget pitching for a minute," he said, then set the ball in Jim's hand. "Just go through the motions of pitching, twisting your hand the way you ought to and snapping your arm down real hard."

That's all Jim did for five minutes.

Back to work they went. It was getting dark. They kept right on. Jim must have pitched a hundred times. It was like pitching a nine-inning ball game.

Each time he pitched, Skinner barked, "Twist it, twist it." Jim twisted.

Then suddenly Andy yelped, "Now ya got it. It's spinning and breaking. Give it more! Give it more twist! More spin!"

Before they called quits, Andy was practically falling on his face trying to reach the pitch that started out down the middle, then suddenly seemed to pause and dart away.

The next day the Phillies went to Brooklyn for an important three-game series. Curt Simmons won the first game 7–2. All Jim had to do was sit in the bullpen, tolerate the stifling heat, and wonder to himself if the Skinner clinic had discovered the cause and prescribed the cure for his troubles.

The second game was even more important. If the Phils won they would go into first place. The St. Louis Cardinals would advance to second and the hated Dodgers would plunge into the third spot.

It was Robin Roberts against Don Newcombe, the two aces, who five times dueled in important games and each time battled like Trojans.

This game was no exception.

The Dodgers were off to a 1–0 first-inning lead when Billy Cox larruped Roberts' second pitch for a home run.

Newcombe pitched magnificently. In the first seven innings only five Phils reached base, no two in one inning. Dick Sisler walked in the second inning, Mike Goliat singled in the third, Eddie Waitkus walked in the fourth, Richie Ashburn clicked a single in the sixth, and Andy Seminick slapped another single in the seventh.

Then came one of the most surprising base hits of the year. Ashburn, a bunter and slapper, caromed a Newcombe fast ball over the right field wall and the score was tied 1–1.

Since Dick Whitman batted for Roberts in the seventh Konstanty got the "go to work" signal.

Here was the acid test of the Skinner cure. For one pitch it appeared as if the Worcester undertaker had embalmed Jim instead of reviving him. Roy Campanella hit Jim's first pitch in the last half of the eighth for a single. Gil Hodges, the one batter in the league who hits Jim with inexplicable ease, popped out. Pee Wee Reese hit into a force play and New-combe was thrown out. Jim pitched seven times that inning.

In the Phils half of the ninth, Bill Nicholson, a sick man who was later hospitalized for two months, banged a home run over the right field fence to score Willie Jones and Seminick ahead of him and put the Phils ahead 4–1.

A three-run lead over the Dodgers, even as late as the ninth inning, isn't as safe as money in the bank. The Bums fight like fury all the time. Konstanty had to face Cox, Gene Hermanski, and Duke Snider, any of whom could wreck him or any other pitcher.

Jim pitched just four times.

Cox was an infield out. Hermanski flied to Del Ennis. Snider popped to Seminick in front of the plate.

The Phils won. They were in first place, the first time since 1917 that a Phils team had been that high in the race that late in the season. The Whiz Kids almost carried Konstanty off the field on their shoulders.

There was no doubt about the Skinner diagnosis and cure.

This was no time for orderly reasoning or retrospection. But had Jim let his mind run back he could bring the inchoate events into a progressive whole—

the job at St. Regis Falls High School, the quest for Mary Burlingame's heart, their marriage, which led to the meeting with Andy Skinner and the spinning lesson he took from the Worcester undertaker.

Mary is now a solid baseball fan. She listens, with intense interest, to Jim and Andy talk over the whys and hows of pitching and holding that ball. She loves the games and attends at every possible chance, often taking their two children, who are already dyed-in-the-wool Phillies fans. She no longer trembles when Jim walks in from the bull-pen. She's just interested, as the thousands of other fans, in what will happen now.

Often asked what she thinks about having her husband play ball, she says, "I married a school teacher. It's exciting, yes; there is nothing like it from Springfield to Philadelphia; from spring-training to the excitement of a pennant race. It's a job like the teaching we started out with, we never forget that; but we love it."

CHAPTER FIVE

A Bird in the Bush

NO MOUNTAIN CLIMBING novice ever found it more difficult to scale a precipice than did Jim Konstanty to climb out of the abyss of minor league baseball. It wasn't only the financial handicaps that impeded him. It was that his playing was never impressive enough to make him an outstanding prospect.

In high school and college he played wherever he could be used, pitcher, first base, third base. He didn't try too hard at Syracuse to be a pitcher, as he was more interested in playing every day. His efforts didn't impress his coach, Lou Carr, who observed, "You can't pitch. You don't know how to pivot on the mound."

Even on summer vacations Jim couldn't make good as an infielder or an outfielder in small, independent college leagues.

In the spring of 1940, Coach Carr recommended Jim to George Miner, manager of the Massena team in the Northern League. He remarked, "He (Konstanty) hasn't got much ability, but he's got a lot of hustle." The Northern League is an unclassified ensemble. Most of the players are college lads who work in the resort hotels of upper New York State and New England. Robin Roberts, present ace of the Phillies, pitched in that circuit during and after his undergraduate days at Michigan State College.

At first Miner used Jim in the outfield. Jim's ambition to become a pitcher was daily revealed as he pitched the batting practice. Finally, Miner let Jim pitch a game. The big guy had it. He won. He was fast, had a good curve ball, and his control was better than most of the others. The slider and palm ball were yet to come.

There wasn't much chance of being scouted by big league clubs, being buried off in the small towns of this league. It wasn't until "Chuck" Ward of the Phillies, one-time Brooklyn infielder and coach at Rutgers, started making a tour of this circuit and came up with Roberts that other scouts put it on their itinerary.

Leo Miller was general manager of the Syracuse Chiefs. He let Jim work out. Leo took a look at the big right-hander and gave him the O.K. to go south with the Syracuse squad. He spent his Easter vacation at Ft. Lauderdale, under Benny Borgman's watchful eye. Here was a corking prospect. Not ready for Cincinnati or Syracuse but good enough to sign and send out.

That's how it was that Jim turned up with Springfield in the Eastern League the following year. It was his first crack at organized baseball and he was to be groomed as a pitcher. Neither the salary he signed for nor the outcome of his first game were earth shaking.

It's a cinch, that had he not learned frugality as a youngster, he wouldn't have saved much money out of the monthly stipend. He signed with Syracuse on March 31 for $135 a month. The contract stipulated that if he remained with the club after May 10 he would be paid $250 a month.

Jim wasn't destined to get that raise. On April 15 he was shipped to Springfield. On April 25 he pitched his first game which, by an ignominious trick of fate, was the first of nineteen games he was to lose that year. Thirteen of those losses were by one run and five of those narrow-margin losses were 1–0 shutouts.

Those nineteen losses established Jim's first record, a mark which he hastily explains with considerable vehemence.

Hartford was his first opponent. Jim gave ten hits —more than he gave in any string of five games during his banner year of 1950—walked four, and all seven runs were charged against him.

Here's the lineup and statistics for Konstanty's first effort in organized ball:

Springfield	AB	R	H	O	A	E
Otero, 1b	5	2	4	12	0	1
Carlin, 2b	5	2	2	0	5	0
Gridaitis, rf	4	0	0	2	0	0
McWilliams, lf	5	1	1	1	1	0
Robertson, ss	5	0	2	1	2	0
Aderholt, 3b	4	0	2	1	1	1
Torres, cf	2	0	1	3	0	1
Guerra, c	2	1	0	4	2	1
KONSTANTY, p	3	0	0	0	0	0
a-Holtz	1	0	0	0	0	0
Shedis, p	0	0	0	0	0	0
Totals	36	6	12	24	11	4

Hartford	AB	R	H	O	A	E
Eastham, 1b	4	1	0	12	3	0
Kister, ss	4	3	3	1	4	1
Hodgin, lf	5	1	2	1	0	0
Younker, 3b	4	2	1	1	0	0
Bradford, cf	4	0	2	2	1	0
Roberge, 2b	3	0	2	3	3	0
Sheehan, rf	4	0	1	1	1	0
Steiner, c	3	0	0	4	2	0
Suche, p	0	0	0	0	0	0
Jarlett, p	1	0	0	0	1	1
Desmond, p	3	0	0	2	2	0
Totals	35	7	11	27	17	2

Springfield	3 2 1	0 0 0	0 0 0—6—12—4
Hartford	2 0 2	0 2 1	0 0 x—7—11—2

Summary—Runs batted in, McWilliams, 3, Bradford, 3, Hodgin, 2, Robertson, Gridaitis, Roberge, Younker. Two base hits: Hodgin, 2,

Carlin, McWilliams, Aderholt, Younker. Sacrifices: Gridaitis, Torres.
Double plays: Kister to Roberge to Eastham; Shedis to Robertson to
Otero. Bases on balls: Off KONSTANTY, 4; off Jarlett, 3; Struck
out: by KONSTANTY, 3; by Jarlett, 2; by Desmond, 1; by Shedis, 1.
Hit by pitcher: by KONSTANTY, Younker. Hits: off KON-
STANTY, 10 in 7 innings; off Shedis, 1 in 1; off Suche, 4 in one-
third; off Jarlett, 4 in 2 and two-thirds; off Desmond, 4 in 6. Winning
pitcher, Desmond. Losing pitcher, KONSTANTY. Umpires. Arte-
giani and More. Time of game, 1:55.

Several of the players from both teams eventually
got to the majors but none to create the splash Konstanty did. From Jim's Springfield team Otero, Sherry
Robertson, Aderholt, Torres, and Mike Guerra made
it. Early Wynn, a strong pitcher in 1941, has been
with Washington, had a good season in 1950 with
Cleveland. Robertson is now with Washington, and
Guerra, after sessions at Washington and with the
Philadelphia Athletics, landed with the Boston Red
Sox. Hodgin and Roberge of the Hartford team made
the grade. Roberge remained with the Boston Braves
for several years.

The one man on the field in the game who fully
appreciates Jim's sensational rise is Jack Onslow who
managed Hartford. Jack handled that team in 1940
and was fired on July 23, 1941, when his club dropped
to eighth place. Later Jack managed the Chicago
White Sox and got his walking papers there, too,
after constant bickering with Frank Lane, the White
Sox general manager.

Somewhere along the minor league trails Jack and

Eddie Sawyer became pals. Later they were members of the major league contingent of players, managers and umpires who journeyed to Europe and put on baseball clinics at Army camps in Germany and Austria after the war was over.

"Konstanty was a big, green kid when I first saw him," Onslow recalled as he sat in Sawyer's suite in the Hotel Commodore during the 1950 World Series. "He had pretty good stuff and all the 'guts' in the world. I remember when I passed him as we changed sides between innings I said, 'Hang in there, kid. You need a change-up with that fast one you're trying to throw.' "

"Don't worry, I'll get it and I'll get those guys of yours, too," Jim retorted.

Jim doesn't relish that line in the Baseball Register that reads, "Outstanding Performance—Led Eastern Leagues in Games Lost, 1941." His pitching record that year was 4 victories and 19 defeats. He worked in 39 games and pitched 170 innings. He allowed 86 earned runs, struck out 60, walked 82, and finished with an earned run average of 4.55.

In his banner year of 1950, in 152 innings pitched, he allowed 45 earned runs, struck out 57, walked 48, and had an ERA of 2.66.

Toward the end of the 1950 season, Jim and I were chatting one afternoon in the Hotel Chase in St.

Louis. I jokingly reminded him of the lone line in the "outstanding performance" department. This was before he set the record of pitching in seventy-four games. Ordinarily affable and ready to take a slight "needle," he instantly bridled.

"I'll never forget that year," he said. "Nineteen losses. Do you know thirteen of those games I lost, I lost by one run. I can go over almost every pitch of each of those one-run losses. I lost a 5-4 game to Scranton in twelve innings. Then I beat Elmira 4-1 and the next two times out I was licked 1-0.

"Then I won a game and darned if I didn't lose the next six in a row. The first was 1-0, then it went 5-4, 2-1, 4-3, 8-1—I didn't have a thing that night—and 4-3. To win a game I had to beat Williamsport 3-2. That was my third win and it was August by that time.

"I was getting pretty anxious, too. I wanted to be recalled by Syracuse at the end of the year. So to make a good impression I bore down all the way and lost five more games in a row. In twenty-nine of those innings the Springfield team didn't score a run for me. How do you like that?"

If pitching twenty-nine innings without a run joggled Jim, he was told to listen to the tale of Max Butcher, who pitched for the Phillies in 1939.

Max came to the Phils from Pittsburgh at the time

the Phillies had Hugh Mulcahy, Claude Passeau, and Al Hollingsworth.

It was the first time in a coon's age that the Phillies appeared to have a set of pitchers who might get the opposition out. Bill Dooly, then with the now defunct Philadelphia Record, amusingly wrote of them as "The Big Four." The only way each was "big" was in being over six feet tall. Even so, they might have fared a little better than they did had that Phillies team been able to hit even loud fouls. That, however, was one of the teams that would have been duck soup for Singers' Midgets.

Butcher pitched a string of fifty-four innings in which the Phils didn't score a single run for him.

"Seems as if Max should have got a little tired of pitching that year," cracked Konstanty when Butcher's plight was related.

Jim was recalled by Syracuse after the 1941 Eastern League season. Again he wasn't given a chance. He got in only five games and finished the year with one win and no losses. That solo triumph was vitally important to the Chiefs. Jim defeated Newark in the game that carried his team into the International League championship play-offs.

As each succeeding year with Syracuse ended, Jim went back to teaching in the prosperous fruit belt town of Westfield, New York, south of Buffalo. For

the next three years, till 1944, Jim turned out basketball teams which collected a championship or two.
But when spring rolled round, his blood quickened
with the news from the spring training camps, and
the end of school in June found the Konstantys en
route to Syracuse and baseball.

It was a new kind of life for Mary, who had never
seen a professional baseball game before her marriage
to Jim. Back in 1941, while Jim was playing for
Springfield, they had taken in a ball game at Mac-
Arthur Stadium in Syracuse, one of the few they
have seen together. The field seemed at least as big
then as her first glimpse of Yankee Stadium was in
1950. Jim pointed to the green, well-kept field and
the Chiefs going through batting practice, and said
to Mary, "Someday I'll be out there playing."

The year 1943 wasn't productive of either victories or improved finances. Jim was wondering if he
was slated for much of a future in baseball. But Leo
Miller raised Jim's salary in 1944 and hinted that Cincinnati would probably take up his contract. Here
was the chance he had worked for—a shot at the
majors.

It was a determined Konstanty who started the
1944 season. No longer did he lose games by one run.
Of the fourteen games he pitched for Syracuse at the
beginning of the year, he won eight and lost six and

during one stretch had a run of six straight victories.

He had retired from teaching entirely in March, and for the first time had the benefit of a full month of conditioning at the spring training camp. Close friends advised Jim against giving up the security of teaching for a will-o'-the-wisp baseball trail, but Jim was still sure baseball had a place for him.

What happened with the Cincinnati club, and was subsequently duplicated by the Boston Braves, was what Jim calls "just baseball."

However, the Cincinnati action isn't completely opaque. Bill McKechnie managed the Reds. It was the seventh straight year the Reds were a first division club. In 1939 and 1940 they won pennants and in 1940 they defeated Detroit for the World Championship. The days of the great pitchers, Paul Derringer and Bucky Walters, were practically over, although Walters was good enough to win twenty-three games that year.

McKechnie never especially favored rookies. He preferred playing veterans even if they were slightly over the top of their form. The best example of The Deacon's preference for old timers who knew how to play was in signing Al Simmons at the tail end of the '39 season. Al was past thirty-six. Simmons not only played an important part as a pinch hitter but was used in the World Series.

It was the same way in 1925 when The Deacon led Pittsburgh to a pennant. His pitchers on that team were Lee Meadows, Johnny Morrison, Vic Aldridge, and Ray Kremer. In 1928 his St. Louis Cardinal pitching staff included 41-year-old Grover Cleveland Alexander, Freddy Frankhouse, Jess Haines, Syl Johnson, Clarence Mitchell, Wee Willie Sherdel, and Flint Rhem as the baby of the lot. Wotta baby!

The 1939–1940 Cincinnati team depended on Derringer and Walters along with "Milkman Jim" Turner, Milt Shoffner, Elmer Riddle, Whitey Moore, and "Junior" Gene Thompson—the latter, the only youngster welcomed by The Deacon.

When Jim joined Cincinnati in 1944 from Syracuse, although he was twenty-seven years old, he lacked the polish of the veterans. But he did win six games while losing four out of the 20 he worked in and the 113 innings he pitched.

The year 1945 was a blackout in Jim's baseball career. He spent those 365 days plus a few others at the Sampson Naval Training Station, finishing his war service in time to go to training camp with the Reds in 1946.

Then came another jolt. The day the '46 season opened Jim and a bundle of cash were shipped to Boston in exchange for Max West, a hard-hitting outfielder, who promptly stopped hitting.

Jim wasn't in Boston long enough to interpret New England's "Let's pa'ak the ca'ah and go to the ba'ah." In ten games he pitched fifteen innings for one loss which won him a ticket to Toronto. What looked like poison at that moment turned out to be filet mignon, for it was the stepping stone to fame with the Phillies.

That was the year Andy Skinner's spinning theory became practical and the Konstanty slider was born.

Jim's improvement wasn't meteoric. In 1946 he won four games and lost nine; the following year he garnered his largest number of minor league victories —13—and lost the same number, and in 1948, working his greatest number of games in any minor league year—46—his record was again even-steven, 10 wins and 10 losses.

But between Skinner's scheming and Sawyer's serenity, Jim was out of the woods—or rather, the bushes—for keeps.

CHAPTER SIX

The Assembly Job

BEING PROMOTED to the majors, especially to Philadelphia, was no guarantee that Konstanty was going to remain in the big show any more than he had in the past.

True, he had his No. 1 benefactor, Eddie Sawyer, back of him. Eddie realized that Jim carried a well-worn "chip-on-his-shoulder," and proceeded to dispose of it. In bringing Jim to Philadelphia, amidst raising of eyebrows at such a choice, Eddie strengthened Jim's faith in him.

Philadelphia is a strange city. Persons from other less inhibited sections of the country use more definitive and scurrilous terms to describe the city where an elderly male resident is alleged to have shot a letter carrier thinking he was a Confederate soldier.

Philadelphians never impulsively set out the welcome for a stranger, regardless of his sphere of endeavor, except perhaps in the case of a visiting English lecturer. It isn't that they are anxious to hear what an itinerant Briton might have to say. Their desire is to be exposed to his accent.

Actors dread opening a show in Philadelphia. It was John Barrymore who once cracked, "Philadelphia audiences eat their young." Barrymore had more than a passing acquaintance with the city. He spent many years there. In fact, after he became "The Great Profile" there were some who claimed him as their own.

Such great plays as *Desire under the Elms* or *Mourning Becomes Electra* down to more modern vehicles like *Glass Menagerie* open in Philadelphia before a collection of cold, condescending, arrogant clinicians who dare the cast to make them applaud. But let a few old theatrical war horses like *Student Prince*, *Desert Song*, *Rose Marie*, or anything by Gilbert and Sullivan be freighted into the Quaker City and there's standing room only. *Uncle Tom's Cabin* does well, too.

The only boxing claim to fame in the City of Brotherly Love is that the first Dempsey-Tunney fight was staged there. Even now it is spoken of as if it occurred a few weeks ago.

There is no night life in what is sometimes called "The City of Homes." Henny Youngman, Milton

Berle, Sid Caesar, and Jimmy Durante are "sim-pleh devastatin'" on television, but any and all of them would play to spotless tablecloths in the sad imitations of night clubs.

Same way with baseball. There may be a logical reason for the fans' indifference. They've seen too many heralded should-be stars arrive and turn out to be eighth-place stumblebums.

The best example of how Philadelphia fans turn out for a proved star, despite his antiquity, occurred in 1928 when Connie Mack annexed Ty Cobb to his Athletics roster. The fans poured into Shibe Park by the thousands to see the once fiery meteor of baseball. Yet it took three years for the same fans to get around to admitting that Connie's $100,600 southpaw, Bob Grove, had a chance of becoming a pitcher. They still thought Chief Bender and Eddie Plank were pretty good.

That's the atmosphere into which Konstanty brought his slider and his change-up.

Jim's first contact with Philadelphia was through newspapers and radio voices in the spring training camp at Clearwater, Florida, in 1949. He had been with the team for part of the preceding September but only for ten innings in six games, one of which he won.

Club owner Bob Carpenter and Manager Eddie

Sawyer were inaugurating their Youth Program in
1949, with Schoolboy Rowe, Eddie Miller, Blix Donnelly, Ken Trinkle, and Bill Nicholson—all fairly
well identified in the graybeard category—on the
roster. Along came 32-year-old Konstanty who certainly wasn't in the diaper division.

However, Jim wore his thirty-two years lightly.
Even the pink-cheeked, expensive bonus boys had to
hustle to keep up with him, for Jim with his boundless energy worked hard to be fit. Each day he was
among the first on the field and without any urging
made six sprints in high gear. After performing the
prescribed training routine for the day, Jim pitched
at least twenty minutes in the bull-pen before knocking off.

"Maybe he isn't in the Whiz Kid class," said Coach
Benny Bengough, "but he acts like one—and a hun-
gry one at that."

Looking back upon those dreary days in the minors, Jim now counts each one of them as of in-
estimable value. Along that rocky road he met many
of the players he was again to meet and defy, sometimes completely vanquish, as he became the most
important single part of the Phillies' 1950 pennant-
winning machine.

A familiar face cropped up in a fifteen-inning game
the Phillies won from the Pirates 9–7 in Forbes Field.
The Phillies, with Curt Simmons and Russ Meyer

working the early part of the game, took a 3–0 lead which held until the fifth inning. The Pirates then batted eleven men, made six runs on six hits, and ushered Konstanty into the game to retire Wally Westlake and Ray Mueller and end the Pirate on-slaught.

In the seventh inning the Phils made three more runs. The score was tied 6–6. Konstanty settled down for a long haul against the Pirate reliever, Cliff Chambers, who made a habit of making life rough for the Whiz Kids.

With one out in the tenth, Andy Seminick hit a home run. The Phils were ahead 7–6.

All Konstanty had to do was retire Kiner, Westlake, and Danny O'Connell for his eleventh victory of the year.

Kiner, who had faced Jim back in the Eastern League, didn't like that formula. He hit Jim's first pitch halfway across Allegheny County for his thirty-ninth home run of the year. Again the game was even.

Jim had to pitch five more innings before Willie Jones scored from third base on a wild pitch. That run would have been enough to win, but Jim added to his personal satisfaction by ramming a single to center field that scored Gran Hamner with the "insurance" run.

As the Pirates batted in their half of the fifteenth,

Jim took no further chances with Kiner. The count went to two balls and two strikes. Kiner got a base on balls. The three succeeding Pirates succumbed.

During his years with Toronto, Konstanty faced Sam Jethroe, Duke Snider, Bob Morgan, Jack Robinson, and Al Gionfriddo who were with Montreal. Jethroe is now with the Boston Braves; Snider, Morgan, and Robinson at Brooklyn; and Gionfriddo, maker of the fantastic catch in the '47 World Series against the Yankees in the Stadium, is back in the minors.

At Jersey City were Sal Yvars and Don Mueller later with the Giants; and at Buffalo were Bill Serena, now with the Cubs, and Johnny Groth, crack Detroit outfielder. Jack Phillips, Pirate first baseman, played at Newark. The Rochester club, one of the top St. Louis Cardinal farms, had Steve Bilko, Eddie Kazak, Hal Rice, Chuck Diering, and Johnny Bucha, all of whom again had to face Konstanty in the National League.

Jim's principal source of annoyance in the International League was Hank Sauer, a former teammate at Syracuse. Sauer eventually came to the National League with Cincinnati, just as Jim did. Like Jim, he was jockeyed around by the Reds until he was able to qualify as a train conductor between the minors and Cincinnati. Even when the Reds brought Sauer up for keeps, it wasn't to keep him in Crosley Field. He and Frankie Baumholtz were traded to Chicago in June, 1949, for Harry Walker and Peanuts Lowrey.

Whenever Sauer's name is mentioned in Konstanty's presence, the same story unfolds, "He hit three home runs off me in one game when I was with Toronto." No other player at any time in Konstanty's life ever heaped that sort of abuse on him.

During that banner year 1949 Jim relieved in twelve games against Chicago, pitched a total of twenty-nine innings during which the Cubs scored seven earned runs.

He faced Sauer eleven times, walked him twice, once intentionally, and was rapped for one base hit.

* * * *

Eddie Sawyer had inherited a miserable team when he was promoted by the Phillies front office from Utica in the Eastern League to Toronto. General Manager Herb Pennock correctly believed that Sawyer possessed some magical ability to make players exceed and succeed, even beyond their most hoped-for capability.

There wasn't much Eddie could do about getting runs or setting up a defense with Hank Biasatti at first base, Jackie Albright at second, Vic Barnhart at shortstop, and Willie Jones at third; with Eddie Sanicki, Johnny Welaj, and Barney Lutz in the outfield; and with Vince Plumbo catching a pitching staff of Jocko Thompson, Nick Strincevich, Oscar Judd, Luke Hamlin, Bubba Church, Al Porto, Don Carter, Lou Possehl, and Konstanty.

One or two were expensive youngsters—notably Church and Jones—headed for the Phillies while the rest were fill-ins and amiable antiques.

Upon the few and unexpected times the Leafs got a lead, Sawyer had to have a relief pitcher, for any time a starting pitcher went nine innings and won, it was a modern miracle. Konstanty drew the fireman's job.

Konstanty, as an old timer, abhorred the thought of relief work. There wasn't any money in it. The only guys who got big money were starting pitchers. Look at the guys around the International League. Some were still in high school when Jim made his first bid for the big show.

There were "Cuddles" Marshall, Bob Porterfield, Dick Starr, and Don Johnson who expected to become Stadium worthies when the New York Yankees hauled them up from Newark. There were Bob Kuzava, the Baltimore ace, and Max Surkont and Ken Johnson at Rochester waiting for the big call from the St. Louis Cardinals. At Montreal the Dodgers had a whole raft of pitchers learning to become Ebbets Field show pieces.

That was Konstanty's dish. A starting pitcher.

It was Sawyer who was to open Jim's eyes to the importance of relief pitching.

During one of Jim's first relief stints, he was throwing his best stuff up to the plate but was hit hard and was soon on his way to the shower. Discouraged, he said to his manager, "That was my good pitch that was getting hit out there. I guess I'd better give up."

"You were pitching good ball out there today," replied Sawyer. "There was nothing wrong with you. The hitter was just good, too. You can't win 'em all, Jimmie."

Now Jim looked at his job with new eyes. If the Skipper thought he could pitch winning ball, then he could pitch winning ball. Often his arm felt dead from constant use in the bull-pen. His elbow creaked and swelled, but he learned to throw easily in warming up, to pace his throwing, to save his best stuff for moments of duty. The team was alive behind him— the same men who the year before had landed in the cellar. This was playing for fun—not since high school and college days had Jim felt this spirit on a team. By June, Toronto was in third place, an unprecedented spot for a baseball team in that town. Jim was eyeing his relief spot with new respect.

Midway in that season Sawyer succeeded Ben Chapman as manager of the Whiz Kids. At the end of the '48 International League season Konstanty joined the Phils. At the end of the National League season he was signed to a Phillies contract and listed for the 1949 training camp.

"From the first minute I had anything to do with Sawyer I learned he was on the level," Jim says. "He doesn't say much. He doesn't make rash promises. What he says, he means and that's the way you play for him. He was my lifesaver. That's for sure."

Again Jim's wife entered the script. Mary had been following baseball closely, watching from the stands as the wins and losses added up. Wherever Jim was sent, Mary soon joined him with their family. When Jim decided to start a sporting goods store at Oneonta, New York, in 1948, it had fallen to Mary to get the wheels turning while Jim was in Florida.

She was a good listener when Jim brought home his tales of woe, and sympathized with the tough breaks of the game. Often a game would be lost on a dropped fly ball or an infield error or a bad throw. Sometimes the umpire was the robber. However they were lost, the losses went into Jim's record, so he was responsible, Mary figured. And she began to question the let-down in Jim's pitching in that last inning, which let a man get on base or hit a devastating homer with the bases loaded and led to errors from the team-mates.

"It took some time for him to get around to my way of reasoning. Then he became his own severest critic. Now he comes home after losing a game and inspects his own shortcomings. If I say, 'You did well and might have won had there not been that error back of you,' he more likely than not will reply, 'That error wouldn't have hurt had I not allowed those two base hits afterward. I made a mistake somewhere. I pitched high and outside. I should have been inside on that batter. *I* made the mistake.' "

Although Jim studied physical education and is now an apostle of correct dieting, he wasn't always that way. After the meager meals of his early days, once he got his hands on a fairly decent wage he often ate too much for his waistline. He recognized that weakness and eliminated it. Never again was Jim guilty of overeating before a game. Mary did like to cook, but she and Jim concentrated on a well-balanced diet and a trim waistline.

He had the professional tools. He had the ambition and confidence. His mental aspect was smoothed out. His tremendous appetite was under control and supervision. His whole outlook on life and living synchronized with his mechanical ability.

The Most Valuable Player of 1950 was assembled.

CHAPTER SEVEN

If at First You Don't Succeed

ANYTHING now recalled of that 1949 Phillies season is anti-climax, yet tremendously important and revealing of things to come. For it was the formative year of the 1950 pennant winner.

It was a year of surprising performances, of unexpected developments, and of sudden changes.

To begin with, the Phillies finished in third place, their highest point of endeavor since 1917.

Ken Heintzelman, an ugly duckling pitcher reclaimed from a Pittsburgh house cleaning, became a seventeen-game winner and winner of Philadelphia's Most Valuable Player poll conducted by the *Evening Bulletin*, a victory at the fans' polls which carried with it a $1,000 cash prize.

Harry Walker, who won the National League batting championship in 1947, fell so far off form in

1948 that he was traded before the 1949 season opened.

Once the Phillies pulled a triple play and later became victims of one.

At the Clearwater training camp there seemed to be a million—more or less—young hopefuls galloping around. It was reminiscent of the 1924–1925 Athletics when Jimmy Dykes, then a young hopeful himself, went through a mock ceremony each day of introducing himself to other members of the infield. No A's infield in those days contained the same four men two days in a row.

So it was at Clearwater.

There was a nucleus of identifiable players. Fellows like Andy Seminick, Schoolboy Rowe, Blix Donnelly, Del Ennis, Dick Sisler, and a few others who were with the team the year before. Eddie Waitkus and Bill Nicholson discarded their Chicago uniforms for Whiz Kid spangles. They were newcomers to Philadelphia but had been around the league several years and weren't strangers.

Robin Roberts and Curt Simmons, the two expensive bonus babies, had come to the parent club in 1948. They were youngsters, both a little on the shy side, so they kept to themselves.

For the first two weeks, newspapermen covering the training camp, spent the mornings trying to identify the characters tearing around the park in Phillies uniform. Gran Hamner had spent the '48 season with the Phils. Willie Jones had been up and down in 1947 and 1948 but arrived for permanent duty at third base in '49.

Jones and Konstanty came from Toronto at the same time. So did Jocko Thompson, a stylish left-hander who wears more battle decorations from the Second World War than any player in organized baseball.

There wasn't much to impress the writers although here and there a young player flashed the brilliance that was to earmark the team a year later.

Richie Ashburn, converted from an ordinary minor league catcher into a glittering, speedy center fielder, looked as if he'd have even a better year than he had in 1948 when J. G. Taylor Spink selected him as the *Sporting News* Rookie of the Year. In his first year Ashburn hit .333 and led the National League in stolen bases with thirty-two.

The hard core of the Whiz Kid pennant winner was there but only Sawyer realized it.

Certainly Konstanty didn't make any nerves tingle, nor did he give any indication of becoming the king-pin of all relief pitchers in only one more year.

To begin with, Manager Sawyer let Konstanty, Rowe, Heintzelman, Donnelly, and Trinkle, all veterans in age, follow their own training routines, except when they had to work in turn at batting practice or at prescribed pitching techniques.

Several times in batting practice Konstanty let fly with his slider. When it was right the kids moaned. Then, too, Jim was experimenting with a pitch that he couldn't depend on in the minors.

That was the palm ball.

Rowe had the most diversified collection of freak pitches of any pitcher in the league. He threw a slider, a curve ball, occasionally a pitch like Rip Sewell's famed "blooper," a knuckle ball, a palm ball, and to hear National League managers and batters complain about it, the best spitball of modern times.

Rowe denied the spitball indictment. He was particularly indignant one afternoon when a writer from a weekly publication interviewed him in Chicago. Rowe, always articulate, agreeable and amusing, talked for an hour with the reporter.

At the conclusion, the reporter—not a baseball writer—was intrigued with a story he had read about Rowe's spitball.

"Mr. Rowe, how would you like to go through the action of getting spit on the ball? Show us how you hold it. I'd like my photographer to get a picture sequence of your big secret."

G JIM HIMSELF—*One of the most recent pictures of Casimir*
mes Konstanty, brawny, bespectacled relief pitcher of the Phils
d the National League's Most Valuable Player for 1950.

RELIEF WORK IS REAL WORK—Konstanty cooling off
the clubhouse, after "cooling" another rival of the Whiz Kids.

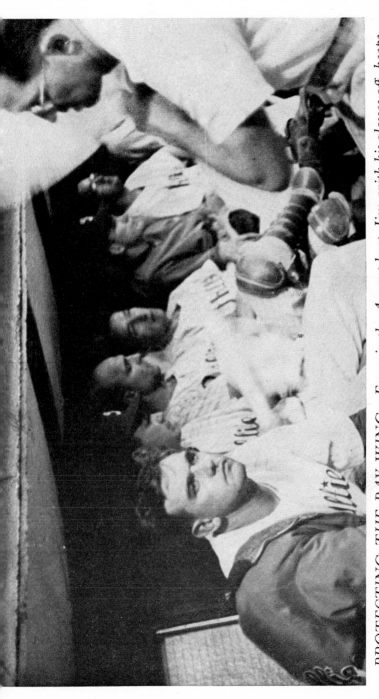

PROTECTING THE PAY-WING—*Even in the August heat, Jim, with his glasses off, keeps his good right flipper covered between innings.*

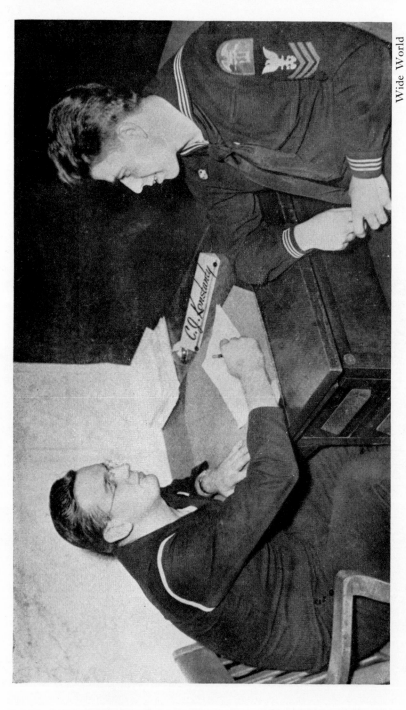

AT SEPARATION CENTER—Seaman 1st Class C. J. Konstanty explaining the educational

HIS IS HOW DAD DOES IT—Jim Konstanty, Jr., eight years 1, explains to young Phillies rooters how his dad grips the ball.

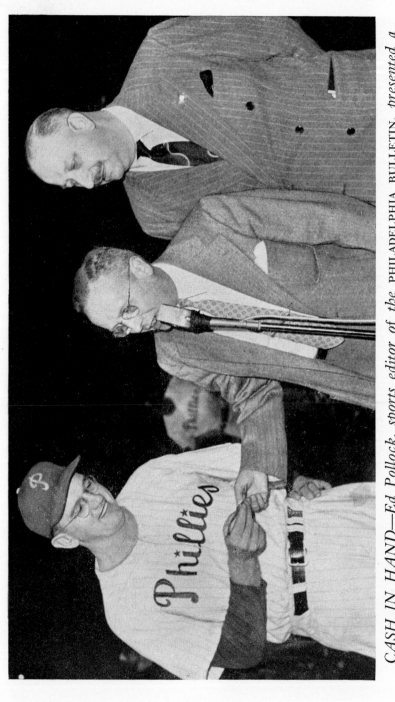

CASH IN HAND—Ed Pollock, sports editor of the PHILADELPHIA BULLETIN, presented a $1,000 bill to Konstanty after poll conducted by paper had picked him as the most valuable big

RECORD-BREAKER—Enterprising photographer gets Jim to se breaking record after he had appeared in his seventy-first relief ore of 1950, setting a new record.

ALL IN THE FAMILY—Konstanty with Blix Donnelly, who received credit for the victory in Jim's seventy-first relief appearance.

THE PAY-OFF PITCH—This is how Jim Konstanty grips his *slider*, the pitch which was mainly responsible for his great work *in 1950*.

Wide World

JUST BEFORE THE BATTLE—Coach Benny Bengough, Konstanty, and Robin Roberts talk things over after final workout before opening of World Series against Yankees in Shibe

THE BIG DECISION—Eddie Sawyer, manager of the pennant-winning Phillies, tells Konstanty, used in relief all year, that he will open World Series against Yankees.

JUST FOR LUCK!—Andy Seminick, Konstanty's battery ma *blows on ball just for luck as Jim tackles his first starting assignme* *in World Series.*

TELESCOPIC VIEW—Konstanty throwing the first ball of the 1950 World Series against Gene Woodling of the Yankees. Catcher is Andy Seminick, umpire is Jocko Conlan.

Wide W

SAME PITCH, DIFFERENT VIEW—Overhead shot of K
stanty's first pitch. It was called a ball. He lost well-pitched game
Vic Raschi and Yanks, 1–0.

OME WITH THE FAMILY—Jim at home in Worcester, New ork, with his wife, Mary, and his children, Jim, Jr., eight, and len, six, just after being notified of MVP selection.

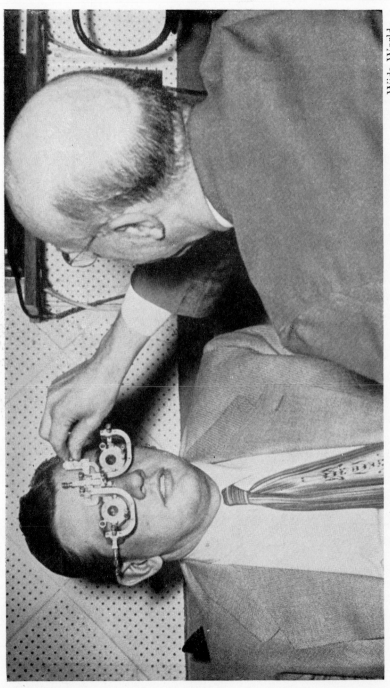

Wide World

LINING UP THE SIGHTS—Konstanty gets fitted for new glasses in annual visit to Optom-

"How would you like to go to hell?" asked Rowe in mock anger. "Mah goodness! Don't you know the spitball is illegal and ain't been tho'wed since way back in the twenties?"

George Earnshaw, one-time great American League pitcher and now a coach with the Phillies, who was standing nearby almost had hysterics at Rowe's reaction.

When the reporter departed Earnshaw coyly chirped, "You wouldn't cheat, would you, Schoolie?"

"No more than you did when you pitched," snapped Rowe.

Earnshaw roared.

"When I was with the Athletics they used to say I threw a spitter," George said.

"Whenever a manager squawked and the umpire looked at the ball Connie Mack stepped in. Because he was an older man and so highly respected the umpires came over the bench when he called them.

" 'I want you to understand Earnshaw does not throw a spitball,' " Connie told the umpires. " 'He perspires a lot. Sometimes the ball may get wet in his sweaty hand.'

"Then he sold me to Chicago. The first time I pitched in Shibe Park against the A's, Connie waited for the umpires to come out. They reach the field from their dressing room through the home team's bench. Bill McGowan was going to work behind the plate that afternoon.

"As soon as Connie spotted McGowan he grabbed him by the coat sleeve. 'I want you to watch that fellow Earnshaw this afternoon,' Connie complained. 'He's got the best spitball since Ed Walsh.' "

"I guess that's what happens to me, too," agreed Rowe. "I sweat a lot out there. I guess sometimes mah hand gets a little moist. But that new guy out there —that Konstanty—he's got me fooled. He's throwin' a spitball as sure as I got two eyes in mah haid but durned if I can catch doctorin' the ball."

. "You're wrong," disputed Earnshaw. "He's not throwing a spitball. He's fiddlin' around with a palm ball. When it breaks it behaves like a 'spitter.' I know he's not cheating. I've been working with him."

The year before when Dutch Leonard was with the club, it was interesting to stand behind him when he was warming up in the bull-pen and watch his famed "flutterball" take off. Leonard threw one knuckle ball overarm, another with a three-quarter delivery, and the third, and most baffling, sidearm.

Earnshaw declared that occasionally Konstanty's palm ball darted and danced as sharply and at as amazing an angle as did Leonard's sidearm knuckler.

This trick delivery was worth inspection.

The youngsters, who were counted upon to become the aces when the Phils headed for a pennant, were strong arm specialists, especially Roberts and Simmons. Donnelly is a curve ball and slider pitcher. Russ Meyer, new with the Phillies from Chicago, featured a good fast ball, curve, and screwball. No one knew what Heintzelman had except good control, a pleasant smile, a thrilling war record, and a southpaw's glove.

When Konstanty worked in the bull-pen he soon had a gallery behind him. The way the bull-pens are laid out at Clearwater, the inspecting writers could stand at the window in Manager Sawyer's dressing room and get a view directly over the pitcher's shoulder for the pitcher's slab isn't three feet from the clubhouse wall.

It was easy to spot the slider. When it took off it was really a darter. His curve ball was quite noticeable and his change of pace cleverly concealed in an exaggerated motion.

The palm ball was something else again. Here and there it worked. It floated up to the plate, suddenly seemed to be fed up with where it was going and zipped away in almost any direction. There were times when everyone was surprised.

Benny Bengough or Cy Perkins supervised the bull-pen activities. Perkins had caught more than

1,700 major league games; Bengough in excess of
1,100. Hence neither expected nor was expected to
be fooled by a breaking ball pitcher from the minors.
The only pitcher who set both of them back on their
heels and made them dislike their assigned tasks was
Leonard.

Perkins, who hasn't a maimed or misshapen finger on either hand after seventeen years of big
league catching, ducked Leonard's practice. Bengough, whimsically, wore shin guards when he
warmed up Leonard before a game.

Like the slider that Undertaker Andy Skinner
helped perfect, the Konstanty palm ball is another
gift. This gratuity came from a one-time pitcher who
never made much of an impression on major league
baseball. It was Ted Kleinhans, a left-hander, who
belonged to the New York Yankees, played around
with one or two other big league clubs, then faded
into minor league oblivion again.

Ted got away with it once in a while. When he
and Konstanty crossed paths, Jim became interested
in the bizarre delivery. Other pitchers used it, not
with any great success. Jim was ready to try anything
to enhance his chance of getting to the big tent. Gen-
erous Ted demonstrated.

The ball is set in a kind of cup of the hand formed
by the thumb and ring fingers. It is held in position

by exerting a slight pressure with palm joints of the index and middle fingers, which merely lap over the ball without actually gripping it. The first requisite is a large hand. Jim has one.

The trick in throwing the palm ball is to keep the wrist rigid and use a pushing motion. The course of the ball is controlled by the arm motion. If it is thrown with a plain overarm motion, the ball breaks downward. An "out" break or an "in" break results from a corresponding twist of the arm, but always with the wrist locked and not snapped as in pitching a curve ball or a screwball.

Konstanty, working on a daily schedule, spent practically all of the training season working on control of slider and palm ball.

Jim looked pretty good in exhibition games and on the barnstorming junket northward. When he got in his first game as the Phils pitcher, Dame Misfortune, like Potiphar's wife, started chasing him.

His first appearance as a Phillies relief pitcher was on April 20 in Boston and he was charged with the defeat. It was almost as lamentable a beginning as in his first game of the 1943 season. He didn't join Syracuse that year until June when school was finished. He journeyed to Jersey City, pitched a one-hit beauty and lost 1–0 when he walked four men in a row in the ninth inning.

Getting back to 1949. He pitched in 53 games that year for a total of 97 innings and finished with a record of 9 victories and 7 losses. Of those 53 games, 15 were corkers. After the Boston debacle he went against Brooklyn with no success, although in facing his nemesis, Gil Hodges, for the first time he fanned him on three pitches.

The next day—April 23—he again relieved against the Dodgers, and continued his International League mastery over Jackie Robinson by fanning the great second baseman on four pitches with two important runs on base.

It wasn't until the early part of May when the Phillies made their first swing around the west that Konstanty began rolling his slider and palm ball successfully.

When the Phils took a 4-3 lead over the St. Louis Cardinals in the eighth inning and Robin Roberts started to fade, Konstanty was called upon to hold it. With one out he walked Stan Musial. Enos Slaughter became the hitter. It was the first time Jim ever faced the great Cardinal competitor. On the second pitch Slaughter grounded into a double play. The Phillies won.

Slaughter then gave Konstanty's pitch—he still doesn't know whether it was the palm ball or slider

—the name that is best descriptive of it. Enos called it a "dry spitter" coinciding almost exactly with Rowe's impression of it in training camp.

As August rolled around and the Phillies were making their big run for the first division, Jim really poured on coal.

In Brooklyn on August 18 the Phillies defeated the Dodgers 9–5 when Konstanty put the quietus on a ninth-inning rally. The Dodgers had their fourth and fifth runs home, Bruce Edwards was on second base, Marv Rackley on first, none out, and the head of the batting order coming up.

Konstanty went to work. Pee Wee Reese went out on an outfield fly, Spider Jorgensen on an infield grounder, and Duke Snider took a third strike.

Then came a pair of rescue jobs in September that were terrific. Konstanty saved games for both Heintzelman and Roberts and almost single-handed pitched the Phillies into third place, although Russ Meyer was an important factor in the last few games.

The heroic performance of September 6 followed a swell job on September 5 that went for Heintzelman's sixteenth triumph of the year. It was a close call, though.

The Giants led 7–5 as the Phillies batted in the ninth. The Whiz Kids, always fidgety and unsure of themselves in the Polo Grounds, suddenly became activated, made four runs on five hits off Montia Kennedy and Sheldon Jones and went ahead 9–7.

Manager Sawyer wanted to let Heintzelman complete his game, but Ken didn't have enough left. Again it was up to James. He had Bobby Thomson, Willard Marshall—now with the Braves—and Bert Haas, a former Phil, to vanquish.

Konstanty pitched five times. Thomson hit the second pitch and was thrown out by Willie Jones. Marshall took a sharp cut at the first pitch and bounced it back to the box. He was out at first. Haas took a called strike then bounced down the third base line. Again Jones got an assist with Waitkus getting all three putouts.

The next day was the humdinger. The Giants, back of Larry Jansen, serenely held a 2–0 lead until the opening of the ninth inning. The Phils tied the score. Konstanty went in for Roberts. Andy Hansen, now with the Phillies, relieved Jansen.

Two more Whiz Kid runs scooted home in the tenth. It was 4–2 for the Phils and a chance to win two in a row in their hoodoo park.

Konstanty had no trouble with Marshall, Thomson, and Haas in the ninth and ended the game with even more aplomb as he retired Don Mueller, Monte

Irvin, and Sid Gordon in the tenth. In all he pitched nine times to retire six batters in two innings. Not a ball was hit out of the infield.

"He could hit you between the eyes with his best pitch and not give you a headache," snarled Manager Leo Durocher of the Giants. "What's that guy got that makes monkeys out of good hitters? He's the kind of pitcher I used to pray to work when I was playing. Look at those good fast ball pitchers getting their brains knocked out and along comes this guy with a 'nothing' ball and wins."

It was a peculiar truism during those few years before the Phillies finally hit the high road to success that at least one player, sometimes two, came through for a big year and helped move the team up and attract the fans at the gate.

From the outset of Carpenter ownership the Phils played electric baseball and raced through their chores, the youngsters trying mightily to make good and the old timers giving their best for that "one more" good year.

In 1946 Frank McCormick ran red hot and hit almost as well as he did in the pennant winning years with Cincinnati. Rowe, getting pretty close to forty, won eleven games and lost four.

In 1947 Harry Walker won the batting championship although he batted in only forty-one runs, and Dutch Leonard finished with a mark of seventeen triumphs and twelve losses.

In 1948 Del Ennis grew up to major league stature with thirty home runs and Richie Ashburn, actually the first of the Whiz Kids to whiz, hit .333 and stole thirty-two bases.

Again in 1949, Ennis was the batting hero, and Russ Meyer and Ken Heintzelman were pitching worthies. Meyer finished with 17–8 on the mound, eight of which were consecutive victories to end the season.

They didn't blow any trumpets or arrange for dancing in the streets for Konstanty at the end of the '49 season but they should have. Maybe it was Sawyer's fault. He didn't toot the horn for any one player. It was "a team" that moved into third place and convinced the National League that the Phillies no longer were dormant doormats.

That year the Phillies led the league in one-run victories with twenty-eight and had twelve shutout wins.

Ken Heintzelman got forty-eight votes in the official poll for Most Valuable Player that went to Jackie Robinson. Del Ennis, Gran Hamner, Russ Meyer, Richie Ashburn, Willie Jones, and Dick Sisler were also mentioned by the twenty-four voters in the eight National League cities.

Not a mention of Konstanty.

Yet of the eighty-one games the Phillies won, Jim had nine triumphs to his own credit and had saved seventeen other games for his pitching colleagues. That was a total of twenty-six games that bore the mark of Fireman James Konstanty, slightly less than one-third of all the Phil victories.

Sawyer was right again.

CHAPTER EIGHT

Sawyer Calls a Shot

BY THE TIME the Phillies were ready to go to training camp in 1950, Eddie Sawyer had taken full command of the team and brooked no outside or inside interference.

Even Dusty Cooke, close pal of former manager Ben Chapman from the days they were ambitious kids in the New York Yankee chain at Asheville in the South Atlantic League, became a Sawyer rooter.

Dusty openly declared that Sawyer was the best manager he ever encountered and forecast that before he was finished the former biology professor would eclipse the deeds of Joe McCarthy, who was Chapman's and Cooke's "boss" with the Yankees.

Sawyer endeared himself to his coaches, Benny Bengough, Cy Perkins, George Earnshaw, and Cooke. Before the 1949 season ended, Sawyer announced that each could have a job with him as long as he wanted it. If there were other better opportunities presented, Sawyer wouldn't blame any one of them for taking advantage of them.

Earnshaw spends part of the season with the team and the rest of the time inspecting youngsters throughout the farm system.

There were plenty of holdout troubles over the winter of 1949 and 1950. Bob Carpenter had just come to own a first division major league club. He soon learned that players expect big money in the years after they have had a good season. That's one of the inconsistencies of baseball. A player may be receiving a very nominal sum and go like a house afire. The next year he climbs into the big money brackets and is a bust.

The first to refuse original terms for 1950 was Del Ennis, a Philadelphia home-grown product who slugs baseballs by summer and peddles stocks and bonds in the off season. Only slightly more than twenty-four years old, this youngster had big money figures ringing in his ears all year 'round. Hundreds of thousands of dollars streamed through his brokerage office in the off season and from the first moment of spring training until the end of baseball the salaries of Joe DiMaggio, Ted Williams, Stan Musial, and Ralph Kiner were daily topics of conversation.

Del wanted more money. He got it, too. His salary

went over $20,000, making him the first player in Phillies history to ring that gong. The highest previous salary was the $17,500 that former club president Gerry Nugent once paid Chuck Klein.

After Ennis was satisfied Andy Seminick, Robin Roberts, and Jim Konstanty had to be met. It wasn't until the team reached Clearwater that all arguments were settled. Konstanty was among the last to sign.

Sawyer, then and now, refused to enter into salary disputes. He doesn't believe that phase of management is within his province, in fact, he doesn't want to know how much or how little any of his players receives.

During the time that salary arguments were going on Sawyer prudently pondered the ensemble he had and the group he wanted. After the third place finish in 1949 he thought he had a chance for the pennant, provided everything broke just right.

Roberts should become a big winner, he reasoned. Simmons had to master control. It was doubtful that Ken Heintzelman would have another big year. The impressive finish that Meyer made in '49 should signal even bigger and better things in '50. Hank Borowy, Ken Trinkle, Jocko Thompson, and Milo Candini were question marks.

Bob Miller, up from Terre Haute—another bonus player—and Bubba Church, out of Toronto, were aspiring youngsters possessed of the proper potentials. Charlie Bicknell, a $20,000 bonus item from a northern New Jersey high school, hadn't shown a thing the year before. There were "Buzz" Bowers, Bill Koszarek, Elmer Sexauer, Paul Stuffel, John Walz, and the veteran Ed Wright, once with the Boston Braves, as remote possibilities.

Then, too, there was Konstanty.

From that layout of pitchers and alleged pitchers Sawyer had to find a winning staff. By the time the season was about to open Bicknell, Borowy, Bowers, Koszarek, Sexauer, Stuffel, Thompson, Trinkle, Walz, and Wright were out of the picture leaving the staff of Candini, Donnelly, Heintzelman, Church, Meyer, Miller, Roberts, Simmons, and Konstanty. Ken Johnson, an erratic left-hander, was later obtained from the St. Louis Cardinals. Schoolboy Rowe had never figured in the 1950 plans. He was given his walking papers at the end of 1949.

When Seminick nursed his money grievances longer than Carpenter thought he should have, there were rumors that he would be traded. Fortunately for the Phillies that didn't eventuate and Andy had the best year of his career. He was the stoical hero of the pennant fight and World Series, playing the last two games of the National League season and all four games against the New York Yankees with a fractured bone in his ankle. Only periodic injections of novocain kept him going.

The infield of Eddie Waitkus, Mike Goliat, Gran Hamner, and Willie Jones knew from the opening of the season that they'd have to play the entire schedule. There were no infield reserves. Buddy Blattner, who had been with the team in 1949, quit baseball for keeps, and Eddie Miller was made a free agent in training camp. That left only Ralph Caballero. There wasn't one prospect out of the Phillies expensive farm system that had the faintest chance of making the major league grade.

It was the same way with the outfield. Del Ennis, Richie Ashburn, and Dick Sisler had to be ready for 154 games. Veteran Bill Nicholson was on the roster. Nick was a sick man, even as early as spring. During the last six weeks of the season he was hospitalized and came dangerously close to going out for keeps.

Back of Nicholson was Stan Hollmig, a $25,000 bonus item from Texas A & M College, a big fellow who had a chance of becoming an impressive hitter but was considerably less than impressive as an outfielder. Later Jack Mayo was recalled from Toronto, and although the one-time Notre Dame track captain is a major league fly catcher, he wasn't ready to face major league pitching.

The lack of reserves was distressing from the

Clearwater outset. Midway in the season Manager Sawyer claimed Jimmy Bloodworth on waivers. The 33-year-old, gray-haired veteran had been around both National and American Leagues. While he hardly fitted into the youth movement, his spirit and will to win made him an ideal addition to the Sawyer scheme. In his drawling, amusing way Jim, who lives in Apalachicola, Florida, said one night, "Goodness me, Ah've had to live thirty-three yeahs to become a Whiz Kid."

Sawyer's plan of campaign was based on pitching. En route northward Curt Simmons proved that he had arrived. There was nothing wrong with his fast ball or curve when he was an 18-year-old lad in high school at Egypt, Pennsylvania. His trouble was control. In 1949 he had experienced a nerve-wracking and severe setback in Boston.

Going into the last half of the ninth inning he had a one-hit victory over the Braves practically racked up. Then Bob Elliott swung at an outside fast ball and belted it into the right field bleachers to snatch the game away from the kid left-hander.

"He didn't lose just one ball game when Elliott hit that home run," sighed Bengough. "He lost ten games, maybe the whole season. Kids can't lose tough games like that one and forget 'em. It wrecks their confidence."

No sooner did Curt start pitching in 1950 than it

was evident the Boston debacle was water over the dam. His control was well-nigh perfect.

The Phillies played only minor league opposition throughout the South and Southwest on the barn-storming junket. They so completely dominated the minor leaguers and the young pitchers got their best stuff over the plate so convincingly, that there never was any doubt the team was well-bolstered in that department.

When the horde of itinerant baseball writers in Florida—Leo Peterson and Carl Lundquist of United Press; Jack Hand and Joe Reichler of Associated Press; John Carmichael of Chicago; Red Smith, Grantland Rice, Joe Williams, Frank Graham, and Art Daley of New York; Bill Cunningham of Boston; Shirley Povich of Washington; "Whitey" Lewis and Gordon Cobbledick of Cleveland; Roy Stockton and Martin Haley of St. Louis—interviewed Manager Sawyer they were told—and sincerely told, too—that the Phillies would be lucky to repeat their 1949 third-place finish.

Sawyer constantly brooded over the lack of a bench.

He feared the Brooklyn Dodgers most of all. He believed then, and repeated his belief before the 1951 training camps opened, that the Dodgers were the best club in the league.

The Cardinals didn't figure too much in Sawyer's

'50 summation. Marty Marion, Enos Slaughter, Harry Brecheen, Freddy Martin, Max Lanier, and Alpha Brazle were starting to show the wear and tear of advancing baseball years. Howard Pollet figured to carry the bulk of the pitching load.

Other than the Dodgers and Cardinals there didn't seem to be too much opposition. The New York Giants, training in Arizona, were revealed only through scouts' reports. At that time Leo Durocher had not dredged Jim Hearn out of the Cardinals' waiver list and Sal Maglie was only a name on the roster.

Many times Stan Baumgartner of the *Philadelphia Inquirer* and I talked about the Phillies pennant chances. When they appeared to be good, they were very, very good. And when they were otherwise, they were unalterably otherwise. Upon returning to Philadelphia, Stan picked the team for a first division finish with a chance of going all the way. In a pre-season prediction in the *Evening Bulletin* I went the whole hog. I predicted the Phillies would win the pennant. Since then I've found it difficult to find a baseball writer who didn't claim he picked the Whiz Kids over the field.

The pitching was sound. With Bengough, Perkins, and Ken Silvestri working constantly with the kids, they had to improve. There was sufficient power among Ennis, Sisler, Jones, and Seminick to score runs. The defense was excellent.

But, had anything happened to the first echelon, both Baumgartner and I could have been as wrong as a Hollywood astrologer.

While Sawyer wasn't as brash in public as we were, he knew what to expect. Ten days before the season opened he wrote a memo, placed it in a sealed envelope marked "Open after October 1" and filed it away. Upon revealing the contents of the envelope after the Phillies won the pennant it was discovered that Eddie had written "The Phillies will win the pennant by ten games."

"How could you have ever written that note when you did?" Eddie was asked.

The question wasn't propounded at a propitious time, for it was asked on Sunday night, October 1, after Dick Sisler's tenth-inning home run had defeated the Dodgers 4–1 to clinch the Phils' first pennant since 1915. Several hours later at the big celebration in Philadelphia's Warwick Hotel, Eddie found time to answer.

"I'll tell you why I picked our team to win," he said, "I didn't want to sound off about it when I wrote the prediction. I'd rather have the young players keyed up all year than have them start out with the idea that they were a cinch to win.

"First I was sure Ennis was going to have a big year. I knew the infield was competent and could make double plays. I thought Roberts, Simmons, and Meyer could become twenty-game winners. Roberts did. Simmons had seventeen games when he was called into service early in September. Meyer was disappointing. He had one of those off years that many pitchers run into. Then Bob Miller and Bubba Church were surprises."

Taking a long puff on his cigar, Eddie almost leered at his auditors.

"Then there was Konstanty, wasn't there?"

For Sawyer had many times hinted that Konstanty, if he came through the way Eddie expected, would be the key to the whole matter.

Konstanty came through, all right. In all the fine performances the Whiz Kids put on during the torrid months of June, July, and August, none surpassed the heroic work of Konstanty. No other pitcher in baseball's history amassed a total of seventy-four games in one year of which sixteen were personal triumphs and twenty-six others garnered for other pitchers.

Ennis had his big year, as Sawyer expected. The big kid hit over .300, slammed 31 home runs and batted home 126 runs. Gran Hamner at shortstop was easily the best youngster at that position in the league. Frank Frisch and Leo Durocher were so anxious to see Willie Jones succeed that they volunteered helpful information to him despite his effort for a rival team.

Richie Ashburn, a center fielder who is alleged not to be able to throw, was a ball of fire all year, and his stunning throw in Brooklyn on the last day of the season prevented Cal Abrams from scoring from second base with a run that would have given the Dodgers a ninth-inning victory. Dick Sisler was a tremendous impetus midway in the year. For more than three weeks he batted over .400. Eddie Waitkus, recovering from the effects of a gunshot wound that almost ended his life in 1949, played courageously and was a physical wreck when the season ended.

Mike Goliat made life miserable for every Brooklyn pitcher. Andy Seminick battled every minute of the year, even with fists when necessary. Little Ralph Caballero, not good enough to make the starting team, became the club talisman. He was principally used to run for some of the slower men in late innings. When the Phils won four or five games with "Cabby" racing home with the deciding tally, the players looked upon him as their "good luck charm."

Even ailing Bill Nicholson delivered in three important clutches. Thrice his pinch hits won ball games. Two of those clouts were home runs. Each defeated the Dodgers. The first pinch homer was on July 2 in Ebbets Field. Ralph Branca was the victim. It beat the Dodgers 6–4. Again on July 8, Nick rammed a drive out of the park off Don Newcombe and knocked off the Brooks 4–1 in the ninth inning.

Not a Whiz Kid missed a cue as the big race barrelled along in those three important months. Had it not been for the lead they piled up during that period things might have turned out tragically different late in September, for before knocking off the Dodgers in the last game, they lost five in a row, four to the Giants in the Polo Grounds and the first of the two-game series with Brooklyn.

The expensive kids took delight when the older players, the veterans nearing the end of their string, came through in tight spots. They called Nicholson "Poppa Nick" and made him take them to the circus in Madison Square Garden. They embarrassed the suave Milo Candini by whispering to hotel house detectives that he was a gunman and racketeer. They made Cy Perkins tell and re-tell of playing against and with Ty Cobb and Tris Speaker. They twitted billiard-bald Benny Bengough about a toupee.

But they looked upon Konstanty as something almost hallowed. Whenever Roberts or Simmons worked, the whole team was electrified. If either of the young aces was knocked out, the team seemed to slough off. Then when Konstanty came in the kids relaxed and knew they would win.

Konstanty became the focal point of all journalistic interest. In Philadelphia he was the darling of the crowds. Even in alien cities the writers paid more attention to Konstanty than to any of the others.

Early in September when his total number of games reached the sixties and it was apparent that he'd break the old record the reporters were after him incessantly. At the ball park, in his hotel room, around the lobbies—everywhere—Jim was the target.

The "undertaker" story was written and re-written. Every phase of his life was of interest. His slider and palm ball were topics for lengthy essays. His inexhaustible energy was a source of wonderment.

When Jim first joined the Phils he was taciturn. He was careful about what he said and to whom he said it. But as 1950 became Jim's "big year" he unbent more, became more articulate, and confident in himself and in his job. His forthright statements sometimes jarred the listening reporters' ears, and one reporter in Philadelphia wrote in mid-season, "None enjoys his success more than Jim Konstanty does." While this was true, it was the only luxury he allowed himself. Jim still plugged along at his six laps a day, his continuous throwing in the bull-pen. He watched his diet, got his rest. The Phillies came first. He made sure that the batter had to hit his best stuff on every pitch.

"That's the reason Jim was successful," Sawyer contended. "He never deliberately threw a 'sucker' pitch trying to catch a batter off stride. He never tried to fool even a .200 hitter. He's not a strike out pitcher. He tries to make every batter hit into the dirt or pop up. He keeps the ball within the strike zone but just about inside it.

"The part about Konstanty that always amazed me was that he invariably gets the good batters out. Fellows like Robinson, Kiner, Sauer, and Hodges will hit home runs off any pitcher who makes a mistake. Jim seldom does that."

"Would Konstanty have another year like 1950?"

"How could anyone expect such a repetition?" queried Sawyer in reply. "Records like his aren't made every year.

"Then, on the other hand, pitchers like Konstanty don't come along every year, do they?"

Fabulous Figures and Feats

ALL DURING the pennant-winning year of 1950 there was a general contention among Phillies players that when Konstanty went to work the better batters fared the worst.

It wasn't that Jim looked upon the lower bracket hitters as patsies. Just the opposite. He goes along with the old adage of never giving a sucker a break. And the .220 hitter is definitely a sucker to good pitchers.

Very often, however, it's this type hitter who makes a monkey out of the effective pitcher. For years Paul Derringer couldn't fool a kid named Ham Schulte who played second base for the Phillies. During the same era Bucky Walters, ace of aces in the National League, wasn't much more than a batting practice pitcher for Bobby Bragan, a Phils handyman who now manages Fort Worth in the Texas League.

The best proof of Konstanty's effectiveness against the better batters in the league is shown in this table, in which the best batters of each team are identified and their records for 1950 against Konstanty set forth:

	AB	H	BB	HR
Snider, Brooklyn	9	1	0	1
Robinson, Brooklyn	7	3	1	0
Furillo, Brooklyn	9	3	0	0
Hodges, Brooklyn	11	4	0	2
Elliott, Boston	6	1	0	1
Gordon, Boston	5	2	0	1
Cavarretta, Chicago	7	2	0	0
Pafko, Chicago	11	0	1	0
Sauer, Chicago	11	1	1	1
Musial, St. Louis	9	0	1	0
Slaughter, St. Louis	7	1	3	0
Schoendienst, St. Louis	5	2	1	0
Marion, St. Louis	7	2	0	0
Thomson, New York	11	2	0	0
Lockman, New York	9	2	0	0
Stanky, New York	10	2	1	0
Kiner, Pittsburgh	10	3	2	1
Westlake, Pittsburgh	9	3	0	0
Wyrostek, Cincinnati	6	0	0	0
Kluszewski, Cincinnati	8	2	2	0

Among those batters, any one of whom could break up a close ball game, Konstanty allowed but 36 hits for 167 times at bat or an average of .216 against his relief pitching. It must also be remembered that almost every time he faced these dangerous men he was in trouble, that is, there were either men on base or the game was in the balances.

In support of Konstanty's own testimony against Gil Hodges of Brooklyn, that worthy is the only batter in the entire league to collect as many as four base hits off him during the season.

Many batters, seeing Jim's slow, darting stuff coming at them, try to blast it out of the park and end up with a slow roller to the infield. Hodges, although possessed of adequate power, makes a practice of just meeting the ball. The surprising success of Konstanty stems almost as much from the batters' inability to rearrange their timing as from Jim's craftiness.

All during the season Manager Sawyer depended upon his strong arm kids as starting pitchers. Roberts, Simmons, Meyer, Miller, and Church operated under a set policy. They were under orders to throw as hard as they could as long as they could. As soon as they showed signs of faltering, Konstanty went into his bull-pen readiness act.

Hence, out of the seventy-four times he went to work there were men either in scoring position or on base in fifty-six trips to the mound. Of those seventy-four efforts he finished fifty-seven games, ending twelve against Brooklyn, nine each against Chicago and St. Louis, eight versus Pittsburgh, seven each against Boston and New York, and five against Cincinnati.

The frequency with which Konstanty relieved is in direct ratio to the selection of Sawyer's pitcher. Since Roberts, Simmons, Miller, Meyer, and Church were ordained to be the regular starters it is natural that Konstanty was called upon most often to relieve those young men.

Roberts and Meyer each needed him thirteen times; Church and Miller each walked from the mound a dozen times to let Konstanty take over; and Simmons, unquestionably the Phillies best pitcher of the year, was seconded nine times by the master moundsman. Konstanty helped Heintzelman five times, Candini on four occasions, Donnelly, thrice, Johnson and Borowy—before the latter was sent to Pittsburgh—twice, and rookie Jack Brittin, brought up at the end of the year, once.

Roberts was in forty games and completed twenty-one for a record of twenty victories and eleven defeats, the first Phillies pitcher to win as many as twenty games in a year since Grover Cleveland Alexander won thirty in 1917. So the thirteen times that Sawyer used Konstanty to replace Roberts is definitely no reflection on the big, strong youngster. However, Sawyer, especially after the Phils got into first place and showed their ability to stay there, took no chances.

As it was, the Phillies participated in forty-six one-run games of which they won thirty and lost sixteen. Roberts had nine triumphs all by the narrowest of margins—all complete games, too—and Konstanty racked up seven one-run victories. Roberts was beaten 3–2 by Harry Brecheen, 6–5 by Carl Erskine, 1–0 by Frank Hiller, and 3–2 by Don Newcombe. The three Konstanty losses by one run were 7–6 to Preacher Roe of Brooklyn in the first game of the Memorial Day double-header when Gran Hamner made a wild throw in the tenth inning to let the Dodgers score their winning run, 3–2 to Dan Bankhead, and 8–7 to Dave Koslo. The latter was one of the costliest losses of the season, for it occurred on September 27 when a Phillies victory over the New York Giants in the Polo Grounds would have clinched the pennant.

Meyer, in needing Konstanty's assistance thirteen times, was smarting through a particularly disappointing year. After winning seventeen games and losing eight in 1949, Meyer fully expected—so also did Bob Carpenter and Eddie Sawyer—to be a twenty-game winner in '50.

In training camp Meyer injured his elbow. X-ray studies in Clearwater indicated a break. Meyer was flown to Johns Hopkins Hospital in Baltimore and more careful X rays there showed a break well enough—but it was two years old.

Somehow, it seemed, Meyer just couldn't get started. He was in thirty-two games but completed only three. His record for the year was nine on the good side and eleven on the black list. Twice he was ejected from games for uproarious displays of temper, a side of his disposition that he sedulously tried to correct. The first time he was tossed out of a game was in the first session of the April 30 double-header with Boston in Shibe Park. He ran into an argument with Umpire Al Barlick when Earl Torgeson was called safe at first in a play on a bunt that rolled between Meyer and Eddie Waitkus. Meyer argued bitterly with Barlick, seemed to throw the ball at the umpire, then bumped into the man in blue. Again on July 26, Meyer had his ups and downs when Umpire Lon Warneke called a balk on him.

When Meyer did show flashes of his '49 ability, he was among the best. He lost six games in a row before he pitched a stunning 7–3 victory over Pittsburgh on June 20, then added a 10–3 lacing over the Giants on July 5. He didn't pitch another nine-inning game until September 8 when he hurled his best game of the year, a nine-inning, 4–3 triumph over the Dodgers, in which he bested Erv Palica, the Dodger pitcher who made life unbearable for the Phillies practically all the way.

Had Meyer been up to '49 standard certainly the Phillies would never have gone into that last day of the season facing dire calamity. The harder Meyer tried to win, the more diligently he applied himself to the task, and the more sincerely he tried to curb his fiery temper, the more fleeting became victory.

It stood to reason that, although the starting pitchers were youthful in years, the Sawyer policy provided for their tiring, especially when joined in bitter battle with older, more experienced pitchers. Roberts, for instance, thrice had to win heroic victories against Bob Rush of Chicago and Ewell Blackwell of Cincinnati. He beat Rush 1–0 on July 25 and earlier in the season took 1–0 and 5–2 games from Blackwell. All of these contests were decided in final innings.

Of all the burly youths Sawyer had, Simmons stood up best. The big country kid from the "Pennsylvania Dutch" region was the nearest thing to "Lefty" Grove Philadelphia fans had ever seen. Simmons started the season by losing his first game, won the next four in succession, dropped a game to the Cubs, then won three in a row. He ran into doldrums early in June but beginning June 27 won six games in a row. He beat Warren Spahn of Boston 3–2, Ralph Branca of Brooklyn 7–2, Howard Pollet of the Cardinals 3–2, Willie Werle of Pittsburgh 3–2, Ken Raffensberger of Cincinnati—a Tartar for the Phils—12–4, and Doyle Lade of Chicago 13–3.

Jim's biggest days were yet to come. Also a phenomenal run of twenty-three scoreless innings, which was interrupted by Ralph Kiner's home run on Au-

gust 25, and then followed by fifteen more goose-egg
chapters for a total of one run in thirty-eight innings.

    This wonderful relief chore started on July 20 in
Pittsburgh. After Gus Bell scored the third of three
runs charged against Konstanty in a game Pittsburgh
won 10–8 with Blix Donnelly the official loser, Jim
retired Danny Murtaugh and Clyde McCullough.
Including those last two Pirates as two-thirds of an
inning here's how the Konstanty scoreless chart
looks:

Date	Team	Innings Pitched	Runs	Hits	BB
July 23	Cincinnati	2	0	0	0
July 26	Chicago	3	0	1	0
July 30	Pittsburgh	2	0	0	2
August 1	Cincinnati	⅔	0	0	0
August 1 (2G)	Cincinnati	1	0	0	0
August 5	St. Louis	⅔	0	0	0
August 6	St. Louis	2	0	0	0
August 8	Brooklyn	⅔	0	1	0
August 9	Brooklyn	2	0	1	1
August 10	New York	2⅓	0	1	1
August 12	New York	4	0	2	0
August 15	Boston	1⅔	0	0	0
August 23	Cincinnati	⅓	0	1	0

    On August 25, when Konstanty went nine in-
nings for the first time and defeated Pittsburgh 9–7
in what was, in fact, a fifteen-inning game, Kiner
hit a home run off him. That ended the string of
zeroes, but in the next fifteen innings Jim went back
on the nothing-nothing standard working against
Pittsburgh, Chicago, and St. Louis, before Enos

Slaughter finally rambled home with the first of two
runs the Cardinals made in the eighth inning on August 30. Even so, the Phils won 9–8 with a three-run
rally in the ninth and Konstanty, sans his runless run,
came out with his thirteenth victory of the year.

Earlier in this chapter it was pointed out that Konstanty finished fifty-seven of the seventy-four games
in which he participated. Since all his regular season
games were in relief, the other seventeen games either
saw Konstanty, himself, relieved or removed at a
crucial moment for a pinch hitter.

In all Jim worked fifteen times against Brooklyn
and during one run of eight games against the Dodgers
was in six. Chicago saw him next most frequently for
he performed twelve times against the Cubs. Cincinnati was almost alien to the ace reliever. He pitched
but five innings in five games against the Reds until
September 15, when Jim tangled in his best game of
the year—the nineteen-inning game, longest of the
National League season—that the Phillies finally won
8–7.

That nineteen-inning game will never be forgotten
by the 20,673 paying customers in Shibe Park's pews.
It was the second game of a double-header. The Reds
had been easy marks for the Phils all year, in direct
contradiction to the sleeping dog act the 1949 Phil
team performed against the Redlegs. Counting the

first game of the double bill that the Phillies won 2–1, the season's totals stood at seventeen triumphs for the Phils against three for the Reds. The Phils won six games in a row before the Reds could win one as the season opened.

The Reds were pretty well fed up being doormats for these brash kids who were at the top of the pile. There wasn't very much love lost between the two outfits, for Manager Luke Sewell had been quoted as calling the Whiz Kids "a lot of lucky, swell-headed guys."

This second game, which was to become a memorable milestone to the Phils, started with Robin Roberts opposing Howard Fox.

Robbie didn't have it. The Reds clawed him for three runs, one in the third inning, one in the fourth and another in the fifth. But since the Phils weren't making any appreciable headway against Fox, Manager Sawyer let Roberts stay on duty until the Phils garnered two runs in their half of the seventh. Robbie went out for a pinch hitter during that flurry.

Jack Brittin tried his hand in the eighth. The young rookie from Toronto took care of Virgil Stallcup, Dixie Howell, and Fox, but when the Phils appeared to be on the verge of a big inning in the eighth, Brittin stepped aside for a pinch hitter. The harvest of runs didn't materialize. The Phils collected one and tied the score 5–5.

That was Konstanty's cue. As soon as that run crossed the plate Jim was on his feet, cranking up. He went to work in the ninth inning. The first two men he faced in the visitor's half of the ninth—Lloyd Merriman and Grady Hatton—hit singles. The crowd moaned. Of course there was the second guess, "Why didn't Sawyer let the kid stay in?"

Then Konstanty showed the Reds what made him great. He retired fourteen men in order until Howell cracked a single to left with two out in the thirteenth. Howell merely was lucky but his luck ran out when Herman Wehmeier, the Reds second relief pitcher, became the inning's third out.

In the fourteenth Jim appeared to be tiring and losing range on the plate. He walked Hatton and Ted Klusewski, with two out. He sneaked by trouble that inning when Joe Adcock popped out to Gran Hamner.

The Reds got a single in the fifteenth, a single and a base on balls in the sixteenth, had no luck in the seventeenth, and then seemed to wreck Jim's little playhouse in the eighteenth. With one out he walked Merriman, Hatton, and Johnny Wyrostek to fill the bases.

Although Phillies fans were seeing the best team in a generation, they couldn't take this with aplomb. Their hero was lettin' 'em down. Wotsa matter with Sawyer? Why don't he get somebody else out there? Yeh? Who?

It can't be said with complete truthfulness that Eddie was sitting back on the bench taking this rude shock with gusto. If Simmons had been available, Sawyer might have sent the young hurricane thrower out to take care of Kluszewski and Adcock. At that moment Simmons was doing "squads right and squads left" with Pennsylvania's 28th Infantry Division at Camp Atterbury in Indiana.

Jim got into the trouble himself. There was nothing to do but let him get out of it. When Kluszewski singled, Merriman and Hatton scampered home. The score was 7–5 for the Reds.

Perhaps Sewell was right when he called the Whiz Kids "lucky." Then again, maybe Sewell and six other managers around the league didn't know what these kids were made of. For in their half of the eighteenth Del Ennis doubled, Dick Sisler singled, Gran Hamner lifted a long fly to Merriman that scored Ennis, and Stan Lopata crashed a line triple to the center field wall that brought Sisler home. Again the score was tied, this time at 7–7.

With Lopata on third, two out, Sawyer took Kon-

stanty out and used Ken Silvestri as a pinch hitter.
Nothing helpful happened, so the inning ended with
the game just as it had been before the eighteenth
started, except with the ante raised two runs for each
club.

And so came the Phils half of the nineteenth. Ed
Erautt took over for Wehmeier. Eddie Waitkus singled. Richie Ashburn beat out a bunt for a base hit.
Willie Jones walked. The bases were loaded, none
out. That's no way to play the Whiz Kids. Erautt
found that out instanter. Del Ennis lined a single into
left, Waitkus came home, and the Phils had their 8–7
triumph in the season's longest game.

The nine innings that Konstanty pitched against
the Pirates and won, the ten innings he worked
against the Reds in this thrilling nineteen-inning victory, more than convinced Manager Sawyer that Jim
could go nine innings at any time. Grant Doherty, a
newcomer as a baseball writer, wrote in the *Philadelphia Daily News* a day or two later that Manager
Sawyer was considering Konstanty as a starting
pitcher. Actually Eddie wasn't at that moment, but
Doherty, seeing through a dark glass, clearly heralded
the move Sawyer later made.

That was when Eddie started Konstanty in the
first game of the 1950 World Series.

CHAPTER TEN

Setback and Success in September

THERE'S an old saying, equally as true as it is ancient, that anyone who can live in Philadelphia climate the year 'round can live anywhere in the world and never be even faintly distressed. In the case of everyone connected with the Phillies that saying was amended to read, "Anyone who could live with the Phillies during the month of September, 1950, could live through any and all vicissitudes and never suffer nerve strain."

As the final month of the season started the Phils were sitting pretty. Prettier than any team since 1915. Only Pat Moran, who managed the last pennant-winning Phillies, sat in the driver's seat that late in the year. The city, itself, had gone ga-ga over the Whiz Kids. They had maintained a goodly lead through July and August and went into the last month with the cheers and sympathy of the whole baseball world, except Brooklyn, supporting them.

As they swung through one city after another their opponents gave their best, trying to knock off the leaders. When the Phils took two out of three games from a club, the rival manager and many of the players said about the same thing, "We gave you the best we had. It wasn't good enough. Now go ahead and win all the way."

Manager Sawyer never counted the team definitely "in." Although he had selected his crew to win before the season opened, he knew his inexperienced, excitable kids were tiring. The strain had been terrific. Eddie maintained a serene exterior even if he occasionally realized inwardly the fight was veering away from him.

"We'll be all right," Eddie declared, "provided Konstanty can keep going."

In one way it wasn't surprising that Sawyer bet his pennant on Jim. At first there was a disposition to make Del Ennis and his terrific hitting the key man. Then there was the superb job Andy Seminick had done behind the plate. Gran Hamner and Mike Goliat around second base had been a bulwark on defense, especially in making double plays. Richie Ashburn's center fielding was terrific. Dick Sisler's power hitting, beginning in early May and extending until the early part of July, had won many a ball game, especially from the St. Louis Cardinals.

It wasn't reasonable to expect Konstanty to keep going the way he had. By September he had pitched in fifty-nine games. He started off with four relief jobs in April, stepped up to thirteen in May, dropped off one to twelve in June, then knocked off fifteen in July, and the same number in August. Until then he had won thirteen and lost four and saved twenty-three.

It was obvious that Roberts was tired; Simmons was headed for the Army; Miller, one of the surprising first year youngsters, was carrying around an ailing arm; halfway through the month Church was to be hit under the eye with a line drive by Ted Kluszewski of Cincinnati and hospitalized; Meyer was depressed and disappointed; Heintzelman had only occasionally shown 1949 effectiveness; Donnelly and Candini could be the aces in the hole—or at least in the bull-pen.

Donnelly had worked so infrequently that one afternoon when he was called from the bull-pen and was en route to the mound, he stopped by third base and asked Umpire Larry Goetz, "Will you please show me the way to the mound? I've forgotten how to get out there."

Not only was the team on the verge of a bust-up but the schedule was formidable. The Dodgers put on a last ditch drive and the New York Giants, with

Jim Hearn and Sal Maglie mastering the Phils at every turn, were on the warpath.

There were twenty-eight games remaining, divided thus: with Boston, seven games; Brooklyn, seven; New York, six; St. Louis, two; Chicago, two; Cincinnati, three; and Pittsburgh, one.

The experts—and every frenzied fan in the city became one—went through involved mathematics, working out unbeatable equations, all proving that the Phils were a shoo-in. They figured the western teams would be easy; that a split with New York was the worst that could be expected; and that Boston was just another club, slightly more dangerous than the westerners. The big test would be Brooklyn and at that point even the Dodgers weren't especially troublesome. Mathematics prove innumerable things on paper. Unfortunately for the figure filberts, baseball, especially pennant-winning baseball, isn't played on paper or with logarithms, sines, cosines, or differentials.

The way the Phils started out on the first day of September made the mathematicians cocky. Bubba Church beat Boston 7–3 and on the second day of the month Curt Simmons pitched a corking game to beat the Braves and Johnny Sain 2–0.

That took care of the first series. In came the Giants to Shibe Park. Robin Roberts was rested.

Robbie had eighteen victories and was easily the best young right-handed pitcher in the majors.

Jim Hearn opposed Robbie. The Phils hadn't licked the Cardinal castoff all year. There was gossip that Eddie Dyer was to lose his job managing the Cardinals for letting Hearn get away. Dyer lost his job at the end of the season but whether the Hearn sale was the cause is a matter that only Fred Saigh, president of the Red Birds, can answer.

At any rate Hearn, just a so-so pitcher with the Cards, became Leo Durocher's No. 1 boy. When he and Roberts tied up in a whiz-bang ball game on September 4, in the first game of the Labor Day double-header, Hearn not only continued his mastery of the Whiz Kids but brought Konstanty into his first of fifteen more actions for September.

Roberts pitched a masterful game. Hearn even more so. The Giants won 2–0. Konstanty, getting into the game in the ninth inning after Roberts was relieved for a pinch hitter, faced Bobby Thomson, Hearn, and Eddie Stanky. He vanquished them with ease but the ball game was irretrievably lost.

The second game was a shambles. Miller, Meyer, Heintzelman, rookie Steve Ridzik, and Candini worked for the Phils as Sal Maglie tossed a 9–0 shutout. Counting the game that Simmons won from Boston, in which the Phils' two runs were made in the fourth inning, the Whiz Kids ended Labor Day with twenty-two scoreless innings back of them.

Of the fifty-four putouts the Giants had to make in the Labor Day double-header, thirty were made by infielders, twenty-one were easy pop flies to the out-field, and three were strikeouts. The Phils made fourteen hits against Hearn and Maglie—five off the former, nine off the latter—and not one was for ex-tra bases, in fact, two were infield hits.

But here came the Dodgers for four games. The Giants were merely running hot trying to insure a first division finish. It was the Dodgers who had to be knocked off, and until that time the Phils had little trouble with the Flatbush Follies.

Church went back to work. He pitched a beauti-ful game. Only Don Newcombe was better. This was the first game of a twi-night double-header and 32,-279 cash customers were jammed into Shibe Park.

The Dodgers took a 1–0 lead in the first inning. That wasn't alarming for it was generally accepted around the Phillies bench that any time they could stay close to Newcombe for five or six innings they'd knock him off. For seven innings Don stood the Phils on their heads facing only twenty-four men, three over the irreducible minimum. Actually Don stood the Whiz Kids upside down for nine innings, getting away with a 2–0 victory in which he allowed only three hits—Ashburn had two of them—and didn't permit a man to reach second base. Konstanty got in the game, too, pitching the ninth inning. The Dodgers almost racked up a run off James, too, for with one out Newcombe proved his prowess as a hitter as well as a pitcher by slamming a triple to deep left field. Cal Abrams and Pee Wee Reese obligingly became the second and third outs.

So the string of twenty-two scoreless innings now read thirty-one. Newcombe was more insolent than either Hearn or Maglie, for of the twenty-seven putouts the Dodgers had to make, the infielders turned up eighteen, seven went to outfielders and Newcombe fanned Andy Seminick and Dick Sisler.

Then came the most haughty irreverence of all. Newcombe came back in the second game trying to perform the "iron man" act. The Phillies were in their worst batting slump of the year. They couldn't get enough base hits to beat the Bloomer Girls. However, their run of goose-eggs ended in the first inning of the second game—played under the lights—for Ashburn finally scored a run. Curt Simmons started the second game.

The crowd, intensely partisan, yet punctuated with zany outcries indigenous to Brooklyn, yelped for the Phils to give Newcombe his come-uppance for his swaggering gesture. It looked as if their uproarious demands would be fulfilled, for Eddie Wait-kus hauled home a second Whiz Kid run in the third inning.

Under usual circumstances Simmons might have held that 2–0 lead. He had pitched shutout ball only four days before against Boston and seemingly was at the peak of his ability. Then came the fatal ninth. Curt fanned pinch hitter Eddie Miksis, who was the twenty-seventh man to face him. Reese was more difficult and walked. Tommy Brown rifled a single to left, Reese held second.

That was enough of Simmons.

The crowd went wild as Konstanty trudged in from the bull-pen. Here was what they wanted. Good old Jim. He'd get 'em out of it. Jackie Robinson was the batter. He was Konstanty's meat. Maybe Jackie should have been. He wasn't. He beat out a single to deep short, filling the bases.

Now came the real Konstanty—the Konstanty the fans fancied. He fanned Carl Furillo. Two away and only that Gil Hodges to figure against. All right, Hodges can hit Konstanty. He can't do it always. He'll pop out now. Jim's got to get this one.

But no! Hodges belted a single to left. Reese and Brown came in, tying the score. So now what goes on? Seminick sees Robinson running. He faked a throw to second, then let fly toward third. The ball was beyond Willie Jones' reach. It trickled into left field. Robinson, starting from first, got all the way around. The score was 3–2. The Phils had now lost four games in a row. Konstanty was the losing pitcher for the fifth time and the lead was cut by two full games.

So what?

A five-game lead that late in the year couldn't be overcome. The Dodgers are just running hot. They'll cool off. Who've they got now that Newcombe tried to go both games of a double-header and failed? He hadn't finished the second game. Dan Bankhead came in in the eighth inning and was the winning pitcher.

The Phils found out the next day who the Dodgers had left to pitch. They had Carl Erskine and Ralph Branca. The Phils had Robin Roberts and, again, Jim Konstanty. Can't this guy ever get a rest?

The next day it was another nip-and-tuck set-to. At 4:30 in the afternoon when a whistle at a nearby factory blew, Eddie Delaney of the *Philadelphia Daily News* cracked, "That means those guys are finished work. For Konstanty it means get ready to go to work."

He was right. Shortly after the whistle blew Jim was at work. He pitched the last two innings against the Dodgers. His excellent work was of no avail. The game was lost before he came in and when the Phils appeared to have a rally under way in their eighth, Branca relieved Erskine. Although Ashburn was on third base, none out, he couldn't get across with the tying run. The Dodgers won 3–2. So now the Phils' losing streak numbered five, the second time during the season they had run into adversity that frequently.

Their lead was down to four games.

Things changed for the better the next day when Russ Meyer came to the rescue of his bedraggled mates and pitched his most important victory of the year, beating the Dodgers 4–3.

That's it, argued the fans. They need that win. They're off again. Just a little setback. To substantiate that reasoning the Phils hauled off and beat the Boston Braves next day 7–6 with Konstanty working the last two innings and getting credit for the triumph—his No. 14 in that department.

Twice the Phils had hard luck creep up back of them and slug them over the skull. The first time was on July 24 in a night game against Pittsburgh. The Pirates had led 2–1 until the top half of the seventh inning. Eddie Waitkus, first man up, whaled a home run into the right field seats, his second of the year and the drive that was needed to tie the score. Then came a rainstorm that almost flooded the Ohio Valley. Umpire Lon Warneke had to call the game. The run didn't count. Since enough innings had been played to make it a legal game the Phils lost 2–1 after tying the score.

So it had been on Sunday, September 10, in the first game of a scheduled double-header with Boston. It was Sain against Church. The Braves led 3–1 after the first half of the sixth inning. Jackie Mayo, fresh up from Toronto, cracked a drive over the right field wall, his first major league home run. The score closed to 3–2. Gran Hamner whacked a single over short. The Phils were off on a rally. So down came the rain again. It pelted down in sheets. In torrents. The field and benches were flooded. The ground crew didn't have time to get the entire infield covered. Umpires Scotty Robb, Babe Pinelli, and Dusty Boggess waited for more than the required thirty minutes. There wasn't a thing left for them to do. "Game's off," they signaled. The score reverted to the end of the last completed inning. That was the fifth. Boston won 3–1.

"They have to have a cloudburst for me to get a day off," Konstanty said.

Then came the western teams, a resurgence of the Phils' ability, and four more outings for Konstanty. One of those was the celebrated nineteen-inning game with Cincinnati, in which he pitched ten innings and Donnelly, who pitched the nineteenth, got credit for the win.

Again two losses to Brooklyn, a quick trip to Boston to win two out of three games, and the dismal venture into the Polo Grounds.

By this time Konstanty had worked in eleven games. On September 25 when he relieved Meyer and went on to win over Boston, he equaled the record of appearing in seventy games in one year. Now it was certain he'd break the record. However, the pennant wasn't flying in Shibe Park by any matter of means.

The very minute the Phillies set foot on Polo Grounds turf on September 27 they were bedeviled with misfortune, mistakes, and misanthropy. Everything went against them and they hated the world. They lost four games in a row. Roberts, with aid from Candini and Konstanty, worked the first game. Konstanty bore the stigma of defeat 8–7 in the tenth inning. In the second game of that day's double-header, Hearn was at his inimitable best again, defeating the Phils 5–0, his second straight shutout over them.

Another double-header the next day. First game went to New York 3–1. It was Maglie triumphing over Ken Heintzelman. Second game Roberts tried a lionhearted comeback with only one day's rest. Result: New York 3, Philadephia 1.

Then came an off day. It was a day of as many trials and tribulations as a working day. The lead had been cut to two games. Brooklyn was playing Boston in Ebbets Field. Some of the Phillies journeyed to Brooklyn to root for the Braves.

Bob Carpenter, Eddie Sawyer, traveling secretary Frank Powell, and Scouts Joe LaBate and Chuck Ward were in Sawyer's suite. They rented a television set. For more than five hours they sat with their eyes glued to the galloping tintypes. Thrice they saw the Braves go ahead. Thrice they saw the Dodgers surge from behind. One Boston victory meant the pennant. For the Phils would be two and one-half games ahead with only two left to go.

There was no luck in the Hotel Commodore's television set that day. The Dodgers won both games. The Phils had two left to play against Brooklyn in Ebbets Field. The Whiz Kids were at the season's lowest ebb. They were on such edge that Russ Meyer almost had a fist fight with a photographer in the Brooklyn ball park.

Came September 30. Brooklyn versus Philadelphia. Bob Miller against Erv Palica. Four scoreless innings. Three Brooklyn runs home. Konstanty pitching for Miller. Duke Snider at bat. Crash! A home run over the right field screen. Inning over a minute later. Brooklyn 4, Phils, 0. Phils at bat in the sixth. Waitkus and Ashburn single. Sisler tripled. Two runs in. Sisler scores. Three counters. That's all.

Dodgers now one game behind. One left to play. A Dodger victory ends the race in a tie. A three game play-off to decide the pennant ordered by league president Ford C. Frick. Again the Phils back of a five-game losing streak. All that was needed on the Phils' dressing room door was crepe and forget-me-nots.

The pennant-winning game on October 1 went to the Whiz Kids in the tenth inning on Sisler's home run with Waitkus and Ashburn on base. The victory was Roberts' twentieth of the year.

No Konstanty in that game.

Jim had done the best he could in that month of travail. Of the twenty-eight games the Phils played they won twelve, lost sixteen. Jim, for the third straight month, worked in fifteen games. That made the total of seventy-four for the year. In September he relieved five times against Brooklyn, thrice each against New York and Boston, and once each versus St. Louis, Cincinnati, Pittsburgh, and Chicago. Thrice he bore the losing pitcher's odium, bending before Brooklyn, Boston, and New York. He received credit for wins over Boston, St. Louis, and Chicago, and did heroic work in the nineteen-inning game with the Reds and the 8–7 victory over Boston.

The new champions—the Phillies.

The finest of all relief pitching records—Jim Konstanty's.

CHAPTER ELEVEN

Glory Even in Defeat

DESPITE the fabulous year Konstanty had, Bob Carpenter ran into no trouble getting him to sign his 1951 contract. That was a surprise in itself, for Jim had put up an irritating argument the winter before.

Upon arriving in Philadelphia for the contract signing formalities, complete with photographers, Jim had something new to talk about. A new pitch, no less.

What it is and how counfounding it might be were academic opinions at that point. Jim amusingly accused baseball writers of naming his one pitch "a palm ball," insisting that he never could understand that designation. Anyway the new pitch is a variation, somewhere between the palm ball and the slider, and is thrown sidearm instead of three-quarters or overarm.

During the World Series, in which Jim was the opening game pitcher against Vic Raschi, he almost completely confounded the New York Yankees. Joe DiMaggio, who went "Oh-for-four" against Konstanty in the Series—had two bases on balls and was hit by Jim—was first to enthusiastically praise Konstanty's ability.

"He's a great pitcher," Joe said in a locker room discussion after the Series. "He has wonderful control, never throws the same pitch in the same place twice, and showed better breaking stuff than I ever saw. We have no one like him in the American League."

There was praise from a real Caesar.

Selecting Jim to pitch the opening game of the Series followed an old Philadelphia custom, a precedent established by Connie Mack in 1929 when Howard Ehmke, practically a castoff, was named to pitch the first game against the Chicago Cubs.

That quirk on Connie's part brought about a situation each year at World Series. While never again duplicated until Sawyer used Konstanty, it always gave Philadelphia writers "a piece" for the papers in pre-Series speculation. It made no difference what teams were contesting in the Series, it would have been unthinkable not to hark back to Connie's surprising 1929 selection.

In Connie's case it was strictly a strategical move. Ehmke was finished so far as the A's were concerned.

He was left behind when the A's made their last jaunt around the league. He was to scout the Cubs as they came in to play the Phillies. Connie knew the Cubs had scouts watching Bob Grove, George Earnshaw, and Rube Walberg. Ehmke believed he was scouting the National Leaguers for the benefit of the three pitchers who were to bear the burden of pitching the Series. Hence he was uninhibited and prepared a thoroughly revealing dossier, so complete, in fact, that Connie, without tipping his intention, decided Ehmke ought to do the job himself.

Before C. Mack could tell Howard his plan, the one-time ace brought up the subject himself.

"I'm about finished, I know," Ehmke told Connie, "but I know I've one more good ball game left. I can lick the Cubs. Let me pitch, won't you?"

"You're my man in the first game. Be ready," retorted Connie.

It was a dark secret right up until game time—that is, a dark secret to everyone but the late John Nolan, then a baseball writer with the *Evening Bulletin* in Philadelphia who had an exclusive story on Page 1 before the Series opened. It was such a stunning selection that Nolan's "bosses" at the *Bulletin* thought he had taken to the opium pipe. John spent several uncomfortable hours until his "scoop" stood up. Had Connie made a last minute switch, the "goat" of that

Series would not have been Hack Wilson, losing fly
balls in the sun. It would have been an occupant of
the press box where the sun never shines.

There was none of the secrecy or surprise about
Sawyer's selection. Nor was there any psychological
reason back of the decision. It was a case of dire
necessity. Sawyer admitted.

Had the pitching staff remained intact from April
until October, either Curt Simmons or Robin Roberts would have been the starting pitcher—probably
Simmons for the word was out that the Yankees were
less devastating against sidewinders than against the
more prevalent right-handers.

Knowing of this distaste for left-handers, some
writers suspected that Sawyer would use Ken
Heintzelman with the hope that the 1949 ace would
have enough to hold the Yanks in check for six or
seven innings, then come in with Konstanty for the
important final innings. If the Phils could get a couple
of runs early in the game, Konstanty would be the
man to hold the victory and send the Phils off with
that important first win.

Sawyer didn't give the experts much time in which
to expert. The team arrived home on the night of
Sunday, October 1, after beating Brooklyn in the
afternoon.

The celebration started on the train from New

York and continued in the Hotel Warwick. Not only did the players and executives of the club take part in the big wing-ding but the whole city went completely nuts. The first noisy salute started in Trenton, New Jersey, where several hundred fans were on the Pennsylvania Railroad Station platform. At North Philadelphia there were more than five thousand at the station, and at 30th Street, where the team unloaded from their private cars, the crowd was immense. It filled every part of the station and overflowed into the station plaza and lined the streets en route to the Warwick.

Philadelphia hadn't turned out such an enthusiastic, yelling celebration since the famed 28th Division returned from the First World War. It took three hours to get from North Philadelphia to the hotel.

It took thirty-five years—thirty-five years of moaning, hoping, almost praying for the Phillies to have a pennant winner. Now they had it. Gone and forgotten were the days of the great Athletics teams. The Phils were in. The dearly beloved stumblebums. Only this was not a team of stumblebums. This was the Whiz Kid team. The red-hot, devil-may-care, onrushing kids who had cost Bob Carpenter more than $3,500,000 in the short time he had owned the club.

Every shop, store, taproom, cocktail lounge, office

building, club, even some churches flew Phillies flags or displayed life-sized photos of the Whiz Kids. They were all heroes. Had Sawyer run for mayor of the city in those first couple of days of celebration he would have won in a walk even against "The More Abundant Life" or against the "you-vote, we-count" city organization.

Only two days intervened between pennant-winning day and the opening of the Series. Manager Casey Stengel of the Yankees almost instantly announced that Raschi would be his starting pitcher.

Sawyer wasn't being "cute" about the thing. He said he'd announce his pitcher at the ball park on October 3, the day before the first game. He did.

"It will be Jim Konstanty," tersely announced the Phils' pilot. And Page 1 of practically every newspaper in the land was emblazoned with the surprise selection. Not once during the season, not once in his sensational run of seventy-four games, had Konstanty been a starter. Only twice had he gone as many as nine innings. What was back of it?

Actually it was a remarkably simple decision. In the last five days of the pennant fight, Roberts had pitched twenty-three innings in three games. Simmons was on duty at Camp Atterbury. Next to these kids the most effective and, certainly, the least excitable pitcher was Konstanty.

He had always wanted to be a starting pitcher. In his own words when Sawyer first made him a relief pitcher at Toronto, "I thought I was all washed up. A relief pitcher was just one step ahead of public relief and it meant next year I'd better start looking for a legitimate job."

After Sawyer's announcement everyone was more excited than the nominee. Konstanty sat in his corner of the dressing room, wiping off his glasses. He and the other members of the team had just finished a morning workout. The Yankees were taking over the field.

"Wotta ya think?" Jim was asked. "You're gonna pitch the opening game."

"Yeh, I know. The skipper told me a little earlier."

"Well, aren't you excited about it?"

"I wouldn't say I was excited. I'm pretty happy about it all, of course."

"Yeh, but this is the Yankees. This isn't Cincinnati or Pittsburgh."

"So what? I have to think of this as just another ball game. I have to think that it's another relief job, only I'm starting in the first inning instead of the sixth or seventh. I've got to make myself believe the Yankees are just the Pirates—the Pirates in a slump."

Jim slept soundly the night before his greatest effort. He was the calmest performer in the dressing room before the big game. Sawyer held a short meeting. The finds of his scouts were again discussed. There wasn't a Yankee player who wasn't fully documented.

Jim warmed up in his regular bull-pen spot, as the regular strip in front of the grandstand was crowded with photographers. This was a good start for a bull-pen resident.

Jim followed his usual technique. He pitched about twenty times from forty-five feet then dropped back to the regulation distance. His warm-up motion is completely different from that on the mound, for he never flexes the muscles of his wrist or shoulder before getting in the game. He merely chucks the ball.

It was strange, but true, that there were no second guesses over Konstanty's being named. Who could second guess a manager who used a pitcher with the record Jim had made during the year, even if he had not been a starting pitcher? The guy had what it took in the clutch and hadn't once faltered or complained of arm trouble or any other disability.

And so the play began. Gene Woodling led off for the Yanks. Four balls. Woodling walked. Two strikes on Phil Rizzuto. Crack! a single to left field. Men on first and second.

"Jim isn't used to pitching with nobody on base,"

cracked Ed Pollock, sports editor of the *Bulletin*. "He'll be all right, now."

So Yogi Berra flied out to Dick Sisler, DiMaggio lofted a foul to Eddie Waitkus, and Johnny Mize hoisted a fly ball to Del Ennis.

Pollock had called that shot, correctly. No runs, one hit, no errors, two men left on bases.

The Phils' batting order was especially set up for Raschi's style of pitching. The three left-handers—Waitkus, Ashburn, and Sisler—were Nos. 1, 2, and 3 followed by right-handers Del Ennis, Willie Jones, Gran Hamner, Andy Seminick, Mike Goliat, and Konstanty. This was Sawyer's usual batting order against good, right-handed pitching. Against southpaws, Jones and Ennis were moved up and Sisler batted in the No. 5 spot.

Raschi, not being a relief pitcher and not addicted to the unpleasant sight of men on bases, started out in the prescribed form of winning hurlers.

All three left-handers he faced in the first inning were knocked off without a ball going out of the infield. In fact, Raschi had assists on both Ashburn and Sisler who hit apologetic shots back to the box.

Konstanty took the Yanks one-two-three in the second, which was the way Raschi handled Ennis, Jones, and Hamner. Again not a Phil could nudge the ball beyond the inner cordon.

In the third Konstanty was back in more familiar surroundings. Raschi clipped a single over short, Woodling walked for the second straight time. After Rizzuto sacrificed and Berra hit a fly ball to Sisler, Jim was ordered by Sawyer to walk DiMaggio. There was a situation to which Jim had become accustomed. Bases loaded, two out, and one of the opposition's heaviest hitters at bat—Johnny Mize. In the days when Jawn was with the St. Louis Cardinals and later with the New York Giants he relished visits to Shibe Park. Many a time he rapped home runs over that right field wall. This time John's intent was murderous but his effort suicidal. He popped up to Jones.

Twice now, Konstanty had foiled the Yanks in particularly advantageous situations. Berra, DiMaggio, and Mize couldn't get a run across in the first inning with two men aboard and Mize again fell down with the bases loaded.

"That's the end of the Yankees," forecast the press box Jeremiahs, "Konstanty's got by two bad innings. They won't get a loud foul off him from here out."

That was a false prophecy, but when the Yanks did penetrate Jim's pitching armor, it was in a style certainly not usually associated with the Bronx Bombers.

It was in the fourth inning. Bobby Brown, the

Yanks' Golden Boy, started the small arms onslaught. He hit a high outside pitch into left field. This was heresy, rank heresy. A left-handed batter reaching out and slapping almost a waste pitch into left. What made it more embarrassing was that Brown sprinted around to second.

A double, with none out. Real trouble. Not for Konstanty, though. The tail end of the batting order coming up. Jim'll take care of 'em.

Jim took care of 'em well enough, but not in his desired way. Hank Bauer hit a long fly ball to Ashburn that let Brown scamper to third. Gerry Coleman, who turned out to be pretty much a sitting duck for Phils pitchers in the Series, banged a fly ball to Sisler and Brown came home. A two-bagger and two fly balls netted the Yanks their run—the only run of the game—but enough for the Yanks to win 1–0, just as they had in the first game against Brooklyn in the 1949 Series. Only the run that beat Don Newcombe in the 1949 opener was Tommy Henrich's dramatic home run in the ninth inning in the Stadium. This run against the Phillies certainly wasn't a hall-marked Yankee counter.

Later in going over the first game Sawyer said, "I fully expected Konstanty to pitch as well as he did. He didn't surprise me once. What upset my calculations was that Raschi pitched as well as he did."

Raschi not only got the 1–0 victory—his second World Series triumph—but he made the Phillies eat out of his hand. He retired the first thirteen men he faced with only two balls being hit out of the infield. The only two hits he gave were by Jones and Seminick in the fifth inning. After Seminick's single to left, with two out, Vic faced but fourteen batters until Sisler fanned in the ninth to end the game. The only Whiz Kid who reached base after the Seminick single in the fifth was Waitkus who walked in the sixth. No pitcher in the National League—even Ewell Blackwell—ever handled the Phils more cavalierly.

In looking back over the Series which the Phils lost in four straight games it isn't surprising that they fared no better. The Series was anti-climax. The emotional zenith was passed in the final game against Brooklyn that clinched the pennant. Before that, in losing five games in a row, the Phils had scored only twelve runs on thirty-nine hits and had twenty-nine men left on bases. That's an average of only slightly more than two runs per game, far off the required average of a winning team.

Of their thirty-nine hits, thirty-three were singles, four were doubles, Sisler had a triple, and Waitkus had the only home run and that one of the "Chinese" variety in the Polo Grounds. The pitching had been relatively effective, the defense adequate, but the hitting abysmally infirm.

The four dependables in the middle of the batting order—Ennis, Sisler, Jones, and Seminick—were at the season's lowest point. Ennis who finished the year with 126 runs batted in went to bat nineteen times during the five-game losing streak in New York and Brooklyn, made five hits and batted in two runs. Sisler had the same statistics. Jones couldn't hit a baseball with a six-inch plank. He batted twenty times, made four hits, and didn't impel one run homeward. Seminick, catching in four of those five games, made three hits on fifteen trips to the plate and didn't have one RBI.

Other teams experienced slumps, even the great offensive Yankee and Athletics outfits, so the Phils batting shortcomings weren't a baseball oddity. What wrecked the Phils was the untimeliness of their slump. They picked the most vital part of their season to tailspin. It not only continued practically all during the month of September but carried over into the World Series.

Roberts pitched the second game against the Yankees and was defeated 2–1 on DiMaggio's home run in the tenth. The Phils got seven base hits and four bases on balls off Allie Reynolds in that game. Only Mike Goliat scored.

When the Series moved to the Stadium on October 6, Konstanty got into his second game and encountered a second heartbreaking episode of the year. It was the eighth inning with the Phils ahead 2–1, two out, the bases loaded with Yankees, and Brown, the villain of the first game, batting for Bauer.

Konstanty knew Brown from International League days. Although the Yank infielder had crossed him up with his two-base shot in the first game, Jim knew he could get Brown out with the proper pitch. He made that pitch, too. Brown hit it on the ground, an easy roller directly to Gran Hamner. This putout could be the ball game. All it took was for Hamner to field the ball and toss to Goliat for the third and forcing out of the inning.

Then Hamner made the costliest fumble of his youthful career.

The ball squirted away from him. Coleman scored from third tying the game 2–2. The other three runners were safe. It didn't matter that Konstanty again tricked Mize into popping out with the bases loaded. The game was lost in the ninth, when Meyer, who went to the mound for the Phillies after Konstanty was replaced by pinch hitter Whitman, allowed Coleman a hit which scored Woodling with the winning run.

That victory in the Stadium sent the Yanks ahead

three games to none, but Konstanty had a third and final effort to make in the Series.

Manager Sawyer started Bob Miller in the fourth game against young "Whitey" Ford. Between an ailing arm and the desire of the Yanks to get it over in four games, Miller lasted only against four batters in the first inning. The Yanks were ahead 2–0, DiMaggio was on second base, one out, and Jim got his final call of the year.

Even then, the Phils playing in the home grounds of the Yanks and with 68,098 clients in the stands, Konstanty got a roaring ovation as he trekked in from the far reaches of the park.

Again Jim turned the trick as it should have been turned. Again it was Mize who became Konstanty's fall guy. Also Brown. They rolled puny grounders to Goliat and were thrown out. Jim stopped the Yankee big inning in the making. It was almost a repetition of the first game so far as the Phils were concerned. Ford turned them back inning after inning stoutly defending the 2–0 lead.

If only the Phils could get a rally started! They did in the ninth inning but it was too late. Just once Konstanty lagged.

In the sixth Berra started things rolling with a home run into the right field seats. Konstanty then plunked a pitch against DiMaggio's ribs. "Not hard enough,"

Joe said, "to have blacked my eye had he hit me there." Brown was up to his old tricks again. He hit a triple. DiMaggio scored. When Bauer lined deep to Sisler, Brown came home. Three runs on two hits and a hit batsman. The biggest inning since mid-July off Konstanty.

So the 1950 World Series ended with the Yankees easy winners over the Whiz Kids.

"They had as good pitching as I've ever seen in a World Series," commented Manager Casey Stengel of the victors. "That kid Roberts ought to be a great pitcher, and Konstanty is one of the greatest I've ever seen in a clutch."

And so the kid who had started work at sixteen lugging 200-pound barrels on his shoulder came into a fitting tribute from a great manager. That it was a well-earned tribute his record for the year shows— he worked in a total of 74 games, four more than the previous record, didn't pitch one complete game, had 152 innings to his credit, 16 triumphs, 7 losses, gave 108 base hits, 50 bases on balls, 56 strikeouts, one wild pitch, 51 runs of which 45 were earned, and had an earned run average of 2.66.

Konstanty had finally arrived as a big league pitcher, realizing the dream of boyhood. Jim grins as he sums up, "And there were guys who thought I'd never be a pitcher."

"But know how I really knew when I had made good?" Jim asked. "It was when I got back to Worcester, New York. The people in Worcester, my wife's home town, now called me Jim Konstanty. I wasn't Mary Burlingame's husband any more."

Appendix

THE MOST VALUABLE PLAYER AWARD
NATIONAL LEAGUE—1950
Selected by the Baseball Writers' Association of America

Jim Konstanty was elected most valuable player of 1950 in the National League and received the Kenesaw Mountain Landis award.

Three baseball writers from each of the eight cities listed ten players in the order of their value. A first place choice counted fourteen points while any man second on a list received nine points, with eight points for a third spot and so on down to one point for being named tenth.

Player	1	2	3	4	5	6	7	8	9	10	Total
Konstanty, Philadelphia	18	3	—	1	—	—	—	—	—	—	286
Musial, St. Louis	1	6	5	3	1	2	1	3	—	—	158
Stanky, New York	2	5	3	3	1	1	2	2	—	1	144
Ennis, Philadelphia	—	4	2	2	4	2	1	—	—	—	104
Kiner, Pittsburgh	1	1	1	1	2	7	—	1	1	1	91
Hamner, Philadelphia	2	1	2	—	2	—	1	3	—	1	79
Roberts, Philadelphia	—	1	1	3	1	—	5	—	2	—	68
Hodges, Brooklyn	—	2	2	—	2	1	—	1	—	1	55
Snider, Brooklyn	—	—	2	1	1	2	2	2	—	—	53
Maglie, New York	—	—	1	2	1	2	1	1	3	—	51
Blackwell, Cincinnati	—	—	1	2	1	1	—	1	1	3	41
Pafko, Chicago	—	—	—	1	1	1	2	1	4	1	38
Campanella, Brooklyn	—	—	—	1	—	1	1	3	1	2	29
Seminick, Philadelphia	—	1	1	—	—	—	1	—	2	—	25
Robinson, Brooklyn	—	—	1	—	—	—	1	3	—	2	23
Simmons, Philadelphia	—	—	—	2	—	—	1	—	2	—	22
Roe, Brooklyn	—	—	1	1	—	—	—	—	—	—	15
Kluszewski, Cincinnati	—	—	—	—	—	—	2	—	1	4	14
Spahn, Boston	—	—	—	—	2	—	—	—	—	2	14
Newcombe, Brooklyn	—	—	—	1	1	—	1	—	—	—	14
Sain, Boston	—	—	—	—	2	—	—	—	—	2	12
Gordon, Boston	—	—	—	—	1	1	—	—	—	—	11
Hearn, New York	—	—	—	—	1	—	—	—	2	—	10
Reese, Brooklyn	—	—	—	1	—	—	—	—	—	1	8
Waitkus, Philadelphia	—	—	1	—	—	—	—	—	—	—	8
Elliott, Boston	—	—	—	—	—	—	1	—	2	—	8
Torgeson, Boston	—	—	—	—	—	1	—	—	—	—	6
Jethroe, Boston	—	—	—	—	—	1	—	—	—	—	6
Sauer, Chicago	—	—	—	—	—	—	1	—	—	1	5
Bickford, Boston	—	—	—	—	—	—	—	1	—	1	4
Furillo, Brooklyn	—	—	—	—	—	—	1	—	—	—	4
Westrum, New York	—	—	—	—	—	—	—	1	—	—	3
Sisler, Philadelphia	—	—	—	—	—	—	—	—	1	—	2
Thompson, New York	—	—	—	—	—	—	—	—	1	—	2
Jansen, New York	—	—	—	—	—	—	—	—	1	—	2
Jones, Philadelphia	—	—	—	—	—	—	—	—	—	1	1
	24	24	24	24	24	24	24	24	24	24	1416

Honorable Mention

Seminick, Philadelphia, and Spahn, Boston, 10; Campanella, Brooklyn, and Blackwell, Cincinnati, 9; Sauer, Chicago, 8; Robinson, Brooklyn, Cox, Brooklyn, Waitkus, Philadelphia, and Roberts, Philadelphia, 7; Bickford, Boston, Pafko, Chicago, Maglie, New York, Hamner, Philadelphia, Slaughter, St. Louis, Elliott, Boston, Dark, New York, Jansen, New York, and Schoendienst, St. Louis, 6; Sain, Boston, Snider, Brooklyn, Hearn, New York, and Kiner, Pittsburgh, 5; Reese, Brooklyn, Kluszewski, Cincinnati, Wyrostek, Cincinnati, Westrum, New York, Simmons, Philadelphia, and Jones, Philadelphia, 4; Jethroe, Boston, and Hiller, Chicago, 3; Torgeson, Boston, W. Cooper, Boston, Newcombe, Brooklyn, Smalley, Chicago, Ennis, Philadelphia, Ashburn, Philadelphia, Sisler, Philadelphia, and Konstanty, Philadelphia, 2; Gordon, Boston, Palica, Brooklyn, Klippstein, Chicago, Wehmeier, Cincinnati, Adcock, Cincinnati, Lockman, New York, Thompson, New York, Thomson, New York, Stanky, New York, D. Mueller, New York, Westlake, Pittsburgh, Pollet, St. Louis, Musial, St. Louis, Marion, St. Louis, and Lanier, St. Louis, 1.

COMMITTEE

Chester L. Smith, *Chairman*

BOSTON—Roger Birtwell, *Globe;* Gordon Campbell, *Traveler;* Robert Ajemian, *American.*

BROOKLYN—Harold C. Burr, *Eagle;* Gus Steiger, *Daily Mirror;* Roscoe McGowen, *Times.*

CHICAGO—John C. Hoffman, *Sun and Times;* Edward Burns, *Tribune;* Dan Desmond, *Herald-American.*

CINCINNATI—Tom Swope, *Post;* Frank Y. Grayson, *Times-Star;* Lou Smith, *Enquirer.*

NEW YORK—James P. Dawson, *Times;* James McCulley, *Daily News;* Barney Kremenko, *Journal-American.*

PHILADELPHIA—Stan Baumgartner, *Inquirer;* Grant Doherty, *Daily News;* Franklin W. Yeutter, *Bulletin.*

PITTSBURGH—Charles J. Doyle, *Sun-Telegraph;* Lester J. Biederman, *Press;* Jack Hernon, *Post-Gazette.*

ST. LOUIS—Martin J. Haley, *Globe-Democrat;* W. Vernon Tietjen, *Star-Times;* Robert W. Broeg, *Post-Dispatch.*

NATIONAL LEAGUE
MOST VALUABLE PLAYER AWARDS

Chalmers Award—Highest possible total, 64 points

YEAR	PLAYER CLUB	POINTS
1911—Frank Schulte, Chicago Cubs		29
1912—Lawrence J. Doyle, New York Giants		48
1913—Jacob E. Daubert, Brooklyn Dodgers		50
1914—John J. Evers, Boston Braves		50

(DISCONTINUED)

League Award—Highest possible total, 80 points

1924—Arthur C. Vance, Brooklyn Dodgers	74
1925—Rogers Hornsby, St. Louis Cardinals	73
1926—Robert A. O'Farrell, St. Louis Cardinals	79
1927—Paul G. Waner, Pittsburgh Pirates	72
1928—James L. Bottomley, St. Louis Cardinals	76
1929—Rogers Hornsby, Chicago Cubs	60

(DISCONTINUED)

Baseball Writers' Association Award

1931—Frank F. Frisch, St. Louis Cardinals	65
1932—Charles H. Klein, Philadelphia Phils	78
1933—Carl O. Hubbell, New York Giants	77
1934—Jerome H. Dean, St. Louis Cardinals	78
1935—Charles L. Hartnett, Chicago Cubs	75
1936—Carl O. Hubbell, New York Giants	60
1937—Joseph M. Medwick, St. Louis Cardinals	70
1938—Ernest N. Lombardi, Cincinnati Reds	229 *
1939—William H. Walters, Cincinnati Reds	303
1940—Frank A. McCormick, Cincinnati Reds	274
1941—Adolph Camilli, Brooklyn Dodgers	300
1942—Morton C. Cooper, St. Louis Cardinals	263
1943—Stanley F. Musial, St. Louis Cardinals	267
1944—Martin W. Marion, St. Louis Cardinals	190
1945—Philip J. Cavarretta, Chicago Cubs	279
1946—Stanley F. Musial, St. Louis Cardinals	319
1947—Robert I. Elliott, Boston Braves	205
1948—Stanley F. Musial, St. Louis Cardinals	303
1949—Jackie R. Robinson, Brooklyn Dodgers	264
1950—C. James Konstanty, Philadelphia Phils	286

*System changed, so that highest possible point total became 336 points instead of 80.

(Courtesy of The Little Red Book of Baseball, New York City)

KONSTANTY, CASIMIR JAMES

Born Strykersville, New York, March 2, 1917

Bats Right. Throws Right. Height, 6 feet, 1½ inches. Weight, 190 pounds.

Year	Club	Lea.	G	IP.	W.	L.	Pct.	SO.	BB.	H.	ERA
1941—Springfield	E.L.	39	170	4	19	.174	60	82	197	4.55
1942—Syracuse	I.L.	5	20	1	0	1.000	9	14	19	5.85
1943—Syracuse	I.L.	29	166	8	12	.400	45	72	144	3.42
1944—Syracuse	I.L.	14	45	8	6	.571	38	44	104	3.21
1944—Cincinnati	N.L.	20	113	6	4	.600	19	33	113	2.79
1945—.........				(In United States Navy)						
1946—Boston	N.L.	10	15	0	1	.000	9	7	17	5.40
1946—Toronto	I.L.	20	143	4	9	.308	47	46	135	3.88
1947—Toronto	I.L.	33	197	13	13	.500	78	62	179	3.47
1948—Toronto	I.L.	46	162	10	10	.500	73	59	163	4.06
1948—Philadelphia	N.L.	6	10	1	0	1.000	7	2	7	0.90
1949—Philadelphia	N.L.	53	97	9	5	.643	43	29	98	3.25
1950—Philadelphia	N.L. (a)	74	152	16	7	.696	56	50	108	2.66
Complete Major League Totals											
3 yrs........	163	387	32	17	.653	134	121	343	...	

World Series Record

1950—Philadelphia	N.L.	3	15	0	1	.000	3	4	9	2.40

(a) Voted Most Valuable Player in National League for 1950.

THE MOST VALUABLE PLAYER AWARD
AMERICAN LEAGUE—1950

Selected by the Baseball Writers' Association of America

Phil Rizzuto was elected most valuable player of 1950 in the American League and received the Kenesaw Mountain Landis award.

Three baseball writers from each of the eight cities listed ten players in the order of their value. A first place choice counted fourteen points while any man second on a list received nine points, with eight points for a third spot and so on down to one point for being named tenth.

The tabulation:

Player	1	2	3	4	5	6	7	8	9	10	Total
Rizzuto, New York	16	5	1	1	—	—	—	—	—	—	284
Goodman, Boston	4	5	5	1	4	1	—	1	—	—	180
Berra, New York	3	5	2	1	2	3	1	1	—	2	146
Kell, Detroit	—	4	3	3	2	2	3	4	—	—	127
Lemon, Cleveland	—	1	3	4	3	2	—	2	1	5	102
Dropo, Boston	—	—	5	2	1	2	—	1	—	2	75
Raschi, New York	—	—	—	2	3	2	3	—	4	1	63
Doby, Cleveland	—	1	—	1	1	1	3	3	4	1	57
DiMaggio, New York	—	1	1	3	1	—	1	1	1	1	54
Wertz, Detroit	—	1	1	1	2	1	1	—	1	3	50
Evers, Detroit	—	—	1	1	—	1	3	1	1	1	38
Carrasquel, Chicago	—	—	1	—	1	—	1	1	—	—	21
Trout, Detroit	—	—	—	1	1	1	—	—	1	1	21
DiMaggio, Boston	—	—	—	1	1	—	1	—	—	—	17
Noren, Washington	—	—	—	—	—	—	2	2	1	—	16
Doerr, Boston	—	—	—	1	1	—	—	—	1	—	15
Mize, New York	—	—	—	—	—	1	1	—	1	—	11
Priddy, Detroit	—	—	—	—	—	1	1	—	1	—	11
Rosen, Cleveland	—	—	—	—	—	1	—	—	3	—	11
Yost, Washington	—	—	—	—	—	1	—	1	—	—	8
Parnell, Boston	—	—	—	—	—	—	1	1	—	—	7
Ford, New York	—	—	—	—	—	1	—	—	1	—	7
Williams, Boston	—	—	—	—	—	1	—	—	1	—	7
Garver, St. Louis	—	—	—	—	—	—	—	1	—	3	6
Stephens, Boston	—	—	—	—	—	—	—	2	—	—	6
Houtteman, Detroit	—	—	—	—	—	1	—	—	—	1	6
Lollar, St. Louis	—	—	—	—	—	—	1	—	—	—	4
Lopat, New York	—	—	—	—	—	—	—	1	—	—	3
Wood, St. Louis	—	—	—	—	—	—	—	—	1	—	2
Dente, Washington	—	—	—	—	—	—	—	—	—	1	1
Philley, Chicago	—	—	—	—	—	—	—	—	—	1	1

Honorable Mention

Rosen, Cleveland, and Stephens, Boston, 9; Evers, Detroit, and Raschi, New York, 8; Priddy and Wertz, Detroit, and Williams, Boston, 7; Dropo and DiMaggio, Boston, and Noren, Washington, 6; Carrasquel, Chicago, Easter and Wynn, Cleveland, Ford, New York, and Garver, St. Louis, 5; Fain, Philadelphia, Houtteman, Detroit, Lollar, St. Louis, and Mize, New York, 4; Bauer, Coleman and Di-Maggio, New York, Doby, Cleveland, Lehner, Philadelphia, Lipon and Trout, Detroit, Reynolds, New York, and Yost, Washington, 3; Brissie, Chapman and Hooper, Philadelphia, Ferrick, New York, Kell, Detroit, Lemon, Cleveland, and Parnell, Boston, 2; and Berra and Lopat, New York, Doerr, Boston, Coleman, Lenhardt, Moss and Stirnweiss, St. Louis, Groth, Detroit, Hudson, and Mele, Washington, Joost, Philadelphia, and Robinson and Scarborough, Chicago, 1.

COMMITTEE

Chester L. Smith, *Chairman*

BOSTON—John M. Malaney, *Post;* Joe Cashman, *Record;* Edwin M. Rumill, *Christian Science Monitor.*

CHICAGO—Warren Brown, *Herald-American;* Edgar Munzel, *Sun and Times;* Neil Gazel, *Daily News.*

CLEVELAND—Edward J. McAuley, *News;* Frank Gimmons, *Press;* Harry N. Jones, *Plain Dealer.*

DETROIT—H. G. Salsinger, *News;* Leo Macdonell, *Times;* Lyall Smith, *Free Press.*

NEW YORK—Dan Daniel, *World-Telegram and Sun;* Joe Trimble, *Daily News;* Edward Sinclair, *Herald Tribune.*

PHILADELPHIA—Arthur H. Morrow, *Inquirer;* Raymond Kelly, *Bulletin;* Edward Delaney, *Daily News.*

ST. LOUIS—Raymond J. Gillespie, *Star-Times;* Dent McSkimming, *Post-Dispatch;* Harry Mitauer, *Globe-Democrat.*

WASHINGTON—Shirley Povich, *Post;* Burton Hawkins, *Star;* Robert R. Addie, *Times-Herald.*

APPENDIX

AMERICAN LEAGUE
MOST VALUABLE PLAYER AWARDS
Chalmers Award—Highest possible total, 64 points

YEAR	PLAYER	CLUB	POINTS
1911—Tyrus R. Cobb, Detroit Tigers			64
1912—Tris E. Speaker, Boston Red Sox			59
1913—Walter P. Johnson, Washington Senators			54
1914—Edward T. Collins, Philadelphia Athletics			63

(DISCONTINUED)

League Award—Highest possible total, 64 points

1922—George H. Sisler, St. Louis Browns			59
1923—George H. Ruth, New York Yankees			64
1924—Walter P. Johnson, Washington Senators			55
1925—Roger T. Peckinpaugh, Washington Senators			45
1926—George H. Burns, Cleveland Indians			63
1927—H. Louis Gehrig, New York Yankees			56
1928—Gordon S. Cochrane, Philadelphia Athletics			53

(DISCONTINUED)

Baseball Writers' Association Award
Highest possible total, 80 points

1931—Robert M. Grove, Philadelphia Athletics			78
1932—James E. Foxx, Philadelphia Athletics			75
1933—James E. Foxx, Philadelphia Athletics			74
1934—Gordon S. Cochrane, Detroit Tigers			67
1935—Henry Greenberg, Detroit Tigers			80
1936—H. Louis Gehrig, New York Yankees			73
1937—Charles L. Gehringer, Detroit Tigers			78
1938—James E. Foxx, Boston Red Sox			305 *
1939—Joseph P. DiMaggio, New York Yankees			280
1940—Henry Greenberg, Detroit Tigers			292
1941—Joseph P. DiMaggio, New York Yankees			291
1942—Joseph L. Gordon, New York Yankees			270
1943—Spurgeon F. Chandler, New York Yankees			246
1944—Harold Newhouser, Detroit Tigers			236
1945—Harold Newhouser, Detroit Tigers			236
1946—Theodore S. Williams, Boston Red Sox			224
1947—Joseph P. DiMaggio, New York Yankees			202
1948—Louis Boudreau, Cleveland Indians			324
1949—Theodore S. Williams, Boston Red Sox			274
1950—Philip F. Rizzuto, New York Yankees			284

* System changed so that highest possible total became 336 points instead of 80.

(*Courtesy of The Little Red Book of Baseball, New York City*)

RIZZUTO, PHILIP FRANCIS

Born Queens, New York, September 25, 1918
Bats Right. Throws Right. Height, 5 feet, 6 inches. Weight, 160 pounds.

Year	Club	Lea.	Pos.	G	AB	R	H	2B	3B	HR	RBI	SB	Avg.
1937—Bassett	Bi-St.	SS	67	284	53	88	17	5	5	..	6		.310
1938—Norfolk	Pied.	3B-SS	112	446	97	150	24	10	9	58	26		.336
1939—Kansas City	A.A.	SS	135	503	99	159	21	6	5	64	33		.316
1940—Kansas City	A.A.	SS	148	579	124	201	28	10	10	73	35		.347
1941—New York	A.L.	SS	133	515	65	158	20	9	3	46	14		.307
1942—New York	A.L.	SS	144	553	79	157	24	7	4	68	22		.284
1943-1944-1945					(In United States Navy)								
1946—New York	A.L.	SS	126	471	53	121	17	9	2	38	14		.257
1947—New York	A.L.	SS	153	549	78	150	26	9	2	60	11		.273
1948—New York	A.L.	SS	128	464	65	117	13	2	6	50	6		.252
1949—New York	A.L.	SS	153	614	110	169	22	7	5	64	18		.275
1950—New York (a)	A.L.	SS	155	617	125	200	36	7	7	66	12		.324
Complete Major League Totals 7 yrs.			992	3783	575	1072	158	42	29	392	97		.284
World Series Record													
1941—New York	A.L.	SS	5	18	0	2	0	0	0	0	0		.111
1942—New York	A.L.	SS	5	21	2	8	0	0	1	1	2		.381
1947—New York	A.L.	SS	7	26	3	8	1	0	0	2	2		.308
1949—New York	A.L.	SS	5	18	2	3	0	0	0	1	1		.167
1950—New York	A.L.	SS	4	14	1	2	0	0	0	0	1		.143
World Series Totals			26	97	8	23	1	0	1	4	7		.237

(a) Voted Most Valuable Player in American League for 1950

THE BASEBALL WRITERS' ASSOCIATION

1950 Membership

President: Chester L. Smith, *Pittsburgh Press*
Vice President: Franklin W. Yeutter, *Philadelphia Bulletin*
Secretary-Treasurer: Ken Smith, *New York Daily Mirror*
Board of Directors: Charles J. Doyle, *Pittsburgh Sun Telegraph*
           John C. Hoffman, *Chicago Sun-Times*
           Rud Rennie, *New York Herald Tribune*
           Stan Baumgartner, *Philadelphia Inquirer*

(Numerals after name indicate year in which member joined the Association)

* Sports Editor

BOSTON

American: Bill Grimes '33, Austen Lake '30, Herbert A. Finnegan '39, Michael Gilloly '48, Robert Ajemian '49, Leo White '49, Sam Brogna '50.

Globe: Jerry Nason * '36, Melville E. Webb '08, Gene Mack '21, Hy Hurwitz '34, Harold W. Kaese '34, Roger Birtwell '36, John F. Berry '42, Robert Holbrook '47, Clifford Keane '50.

Herald: Edward Costello * '42, Ed Cunningham '20, Bill Cunningham '28, Ralph Wheeler '42, Henry F. McKenna '44, Will Cloney '46, Victor Johnson '48.

Post: Gerry Hern * '46, John M. Malaney '21, Robert Coyne '28, Gerald W. Moore '33, Howell D. Stevens '39, Albert Hirshberg '42, Joseph McKenney '42, Paul Hines '49, William Listom '50.

Record: Sam Cohen * '31, Joseph Cashman '28, Dave Egan '32, John Brooks '34, John Gilloly '36, Stephen B. O'Leary '40, Matthew Keany '41, Murray Kramer '48, Alexander H. MacLean '50.

Traveler: Arthur Siegal '35, George C. Carens '14, John J. Drohan '28, Gordon Campbell '43.

Christian Science Monitor: Webster J. Morse * '36, Edwin M. Rumill '30.

Advertiser: Michael McNamee '32.

Associated Press: William R. King '29, Joseph Kelley '46.

International News Service: James Bagley '35, Al Blackman '48.

La Notizia: John Garro * '33.

United Press: Jack Frost '46, Henry Minott '47.
Patriot-Ledger: Roger Berry '50, Linwood Raymond '50.
Telegram (Worcester): Paul N. Johnson '50, Roy J. Mumpton '50.

BROOKLYN

Eagle: Lou Niss * '30, James J. Murphy '20, Tommy Holmes '23, Harold C. Burr '28, Benjamin Gold '40.
Journal American: Al C. Palma '18.
Long Island Journal Advocate: Jack Schwartz * '39.
Long Island Daily Press: Michael Lee * '39, Jack Lang '46, John Powers '49.
Long Island Star Journal: Louis F. O'Neil * '31, George C. Burton '44, Stephen Rogers '45.

CHICAGO

Daily News: John P. Carmichael * '32, Francis J. Powers '17, Howard L. Roberts '35, Joseph Rein '46, Neil R. Gazel '50.
Herald-American: Leo H. Fischer * '24, Warren Brown '22, James E. Enright '43, Dan T. Desmond '45, William H. Becker '45.
Sun and Times: Dick Hackenberg * '47, Gene Kessler '23, John C. Hoffman '24, Edgar H. Munzel '29, Seymour V. Shub '48.
Tribune: Arch Ward * '28, Irving Vaughan '11, Edward H. Burns '27, Howard T. Martin '40, Edward Prell '35.
Associated Press: Charles Dunkley '09, Charles Chamberlain '42, Jerry Liska '45.
International News Service: Ken Opstein '50.
United Press: Edward Sainsbury '47.
Howe News Bureau: John S. Phillips '23, Fred K. Howe '34.
Polish Daily News: Ted A. Tryba '43.
Baseball Digest: Herbert F. Simons '28.
American League Service Bureau: Earl J. Hilligan '38.

CINCINNATI

Enquirer: Lou Lawhead * '21, Harold E. Russell '18, Lou Smith '36, Bob Husted '46, Saul Straus '50.
Post: Tom Swope '14, Clarence Wiese '43.
Times-Star: Nixson Denton * '37, Frank Y. Grayson '26, Walter Brinkman '26, George Bristol '40, Earl Lawson '49.

Associated Press: Claude Wolff '48, Harold Harrison '49.
Daily News (Dayton): Si Burick * '46.
Journal (Dayton): Ritter Collet '47.

CLEVELAND

News: Ed F. Bang * '08, Herman Goldstein '22, Edward J. Mc-Auley '28, Hal Lebovitz '47, Regis McAuley '49.
Plain Dealer: Gordon Cobbledick * '28, James E. Doyle '27, Milton Ellis '35, Fred G. Reinert '41, Harry N. Jones '47, Charles Heaton '48, Ed Katz '50.
Press: Franklin Lewis * '30, Frank Gibbons '37, Robert F. Yonkers '41, Jack Clowser '41, Milton J. Lapine '44, Louis F. Darvas '48.
Associated Press: James Sibbison '49, Richard H. Smith '49.
Central Press Association: Walter L. Johns * '39, William Ritt '31.
Szabadsag (Liberty): Zoltan Gombos '34.
International News Service: Adolph Ponikvar '47, Howard Babcock '50.
United Press: Richard L. Dugan '45, Milton B. Dolinger '47, Robert Morrison '50.
Beacon-Journal: James Schlemmer '47.

DETROIT

Free Press: Lyall Smith * '44, James Zerilli '35, Thomas Devine '42, Robert E. Latshaw '43, Richard T. Thompson '46, Frank L. Williams '47, James B. Eathorne '49.
News: Harry G. Salsinger * '09, Sam Greene '23, Harry F. Leduc '22, Harry V. Wade '22, Watson N. Spoelstra '39, Paul M. Chandler '47, Lee Kavetski '50.
Times: Robert Murphy * '35, Leo Macdonell '27, Charles P. Ward '29, Edgar Hayes '32, Lewis Walter '35, Harold Kahl '38, John C. Manning '40, W. E. Anderman '40, George E. Van '43, George Maskin '48, Robert McClellan '49.
Associated Press: David Wilkie '26, Robert R. Sieger '45, Charles Cain '49.
International News Service: Frank R. Snyder * '45.
United Press: Jerry Le Donne '50.
Detroit A. C. News: E. A. Batchelor, Sr. '08.
Daily Star: Douglas Vaughan '39.

News-Advertiser: Harry M. Dayton '19.
Journal: Thomas Mercy '49.

NEW YORK

Compass: William Mahoney * '50, Herbert Goren '36, Jack Orr '48.

Daily Mirror: Dan F. Parker * '25, Gus Steiger '24, Ken Smith '27, James S. Hurley '28, Fred Weatherly '39, Ben Epstein '45, Clarence Cassin '46, Leonard Lewin '48.

Daily News: James Powers * '26, John Ebinger '36, Charles Hoerter '36, Hy Turkin '38, Leo O'Melia '40, Joseph Trimble '41, William Matthias '41, James McCulley '41, Dick Young '43, Dana Mozley '48.

Herald Tribune: Robert B. Cooke * '38, Rud Rennie '25, Walter W. Smith '29, Al Laney '37, Jesse P. Abramson '37, Irving T. Marsh '42, William Lauder, Jr. '45, Harold Rosenthal '48, Edward Sinclair '48.

Journal-American: Max Kase * '29, Lester Rice '11, Frank Graham '15, Bill Corum '24, Hugh Bradley '26, Harry Glaser '28, Lewis Burton '29, Michael Gaven '38, Barney Kremenko '46.

Morning Telegraph: Ira Seebacher * '35, Thomas O'Reilly '41.

Post: Ike Gellis * '49, Henry H. Singer '23, Bert Gumpert '32, Leonard Cohen '33, Jerry Mitchell '34, James Cannon '37, Edward Wade '39, Milton Gross '41, Al Buck '42, Arch Murray '43, Sid Friedlander '50.

Times: Raymond J. Kelly * '20, James P. Dawson '18, John Drebinger '23, Arthur Daley '26, Roscoe McGowen '27, Louis Effrat '35, Laurence J. Spiker '39, Joseph Nichols '44, Joseph M. Sheehan '46.

World-Telegram: Joe Williams * '14, Edward T. Murphy '19, Joseph P. Val * '32, Daniel M. Daniel '13, Pat McDonough '32, Willard Mullin '35, Joe King '40, William Roeder '45, Lester Bromberg '47.

Associated Press: Ted Smits * '47, Gayle Talbot '32, Ted Meier '37, Whitney Martin '39, Jack Hand '44, Joseph Reichler '44, Hugh S. Fullerton, Jr. '46, Harold J. Classen '48, Murray Rose '48.

Associated Press Features: Frank Eck * '33, Tom Paprocki '31, James Becker '47.

International News Service: Lawton Carver * '35, Pat Robinson '21, Bob Considine '33.

United Press: Leo H. Petersen* '39, Jack Cuddy '32, Steve Snider '37, Oscar Fraley '40, Carl W. Lunquist '42, Milton Richman '46, Fred Down '47, Norman Miller '48, Stan Optowsky '48.

Newspaper Enterprise Association: Harry Grayson* '33, Al Vermeer '45, Edward Mills '47.

La Prensa: Carlos F. Ferro '40.

Il Progresso: Joseph Arrata II '48, John Billi '48.

Daily Worker: Lester Rodney* '39, Charles Dexter '37, William Mardo '46.

Jewish Daily Forward: Jay Grayson '30.

Elias Baseball Bureau: Lester Goodman '19.

Baseball Magazine: Clifford Bloodgood '23.

George Mathew Adams Service: Frank Leonard '18.

North American Newspaper Alliance: John Wheeler '09, Grantland Rice '12, Lawrence Perry '45.

Reuters: Harry J. Hennessy '41.

Christy Walsh Syndicate: Christy Walsh '20.

United Features: John Pierotti '44.

National League Service Bureau: Charles Segar '20.

PHILADELPHIA

Bulletin: Edwin J. Pollock '18, Donald Donaghey '27, Franklin W. Yeutter '38, Jerome Carson '43, Raymond Kelly '46, Hugh Brown '50, Dick Cresap '50.

Daily News: Lansing McCurley* '25, Edward Delaney '30, Grant Doherty '49.

Inquirer: S. O. Grauley '09, John Webster '27, Stan Baumgartner '28, David E. Wilson '29, Arthur H. Morrow '44, Allen Lewis '50.

Associated Press: Orlo Robertson '44, Charles G. Welsh, Jr. '44, Ralph Bernstein '50.

United Press: Russ Green '47, Albert Stees '50.

PITTSBURGH

Post-Gazette: Albert W. Abrams * '28, Ed F. Ballinger '09, Gilbert Remley '25, Jack Sell '28, Jack Hernon '42, James H. Jordan '44, Vince Johnson '46, Dan McGibbeny, Jr. '48.

Press: Chester L. Smith * '21, Jack Berger '25, Fred W. Landucci '32, Lester J. Biederman '33, Paul A. R. Kurtz '36, Harry Fairfield '42, Albert H. Tederstrom '46, Robert F. X. Drum '47.

Sun-Telegraph: Harry Keck * '15, Charles J. Doyle '15, Thomas Birks '29, James Miller '35, Philip Grabowski '39, Jack Henry '42, Jack Burnley '48.

Tri-State News: John L. Hernon * '21.

Associated Press: Robert W. Temple '50, James Holton '50.

International News Service: Troy Gordon '48.

United Press: Rudolph Cernkovic '45.

Daily News: Merril Granger '44.

St. Louis

Globe-Democrat: Robert L. Burnes * '37, Willis E. Johnson '09, Glen L. Wallar '10, Martin J. Haley '21, Raymond V. Smith '26, William Fairbairn '41, Reno Hahn '44, Harry Mitauer '46, John Rice '47, William Kerch '50.

Post-Dispatch: J. Roy Stockton * '22, J. Ed Wray '09, Herman Wecke '12, Dick Farrington '25, William J. McGoogan '27, Dent McSkimming '27, Lloyd A. McMaster '35, Robert C. Morrison '37, Harold W. Flachsbart '39, Robert W. Broeg '42, Harold J. Tuthill '45, Amadee Wohlschlaeger '47, Neal Russo '50.

Star-Times: Sid C. Keener * '13, Ray J. Gillespie '23, W. Vernon Tietjen '38, Raymond Nelson '39, Alvin T. Barnes, Jr. '47, Marion O. Milton '47, William J. Fleischman '49, Robert Devore '50.

The Sporting News: Edgar G. Brands * '28, Ernest J. Lanigan '08, Paul A. Rickart '31, Arthur Plambeck '36, Carl T. Felker '37, Franz J. Wippold '38, Oscar Kahn '43, Clifford Kachline '44, Oscar Ruhl '45, Charles C. Spink '46, Lowell Reidenbaugh '48, Leonard Gettelson '48.

East St. Louis Journal: Ellis J. Veech * '35, A. Edward Hagan '49.

Associated Press: Thomas Yarbrough '46, Allan Merritt '47, Nello Cassai '50.

International News Service: Joseph Oppenheimer '50.

United Press: Stanton G. Mockler '44, Paul T. Dix '47.

Washington

Daily News: Everett G. Gardner * '48, David Reque '45, David Slattery '50.

Post: Bus Ham * '45, Shirley Povich '25, William Ahlberg '47, Morris Siegel '48.

Star: Charles M. Egan * '50, John B. Keller '19, Francis E. Stann '33, Lewis F. Atchison '35, Burton Hawkins '37, Merrill W. Whittlesey, Jr. '47, George S. Clark '49.

Times-Herald: Al Costello '36, Robert R. Addie '42, Charles W. Barbour '49, Robert J. Wentworth '49.

Associated Press: Arthur L. Edson '47, Joseph Ives '49.

International News Service: William J. Kerwin '50.

United Press: Ernest Barcella '37.

Gazette: Jack Tulloch '30.

ASSOCIATE MEMBERS

Fred J. Bendel '25, Hy Goldberg '30, Paul Horowitz '49, William Dougherty '50, Ed Friel '50, *Newark-Evening News;* James L. Ogle '32, *Newark Star-Ledger;* Joseph Knack '50, *Toledo Blade.*

FOREIGN

Pedro Gailiana, *Habana El Crisol;* Humberto B. O'Byrne, *Diario de la Costa* (Colombia).

HONORARY MEMBERS

Boston: Victor O. Jones '33, A. J. Rooney '21, Ford Sawyer '21, Les Stout '24.

Brooklyn: Frank C. Ferguson, Clinton Hoard '18, William McCullough '29, Harold Parrott '34, Joseph L. Roberts '28, Murray Robinson '23, Lee Scott '27, Len F. Wooster '09.

Chicago: Will Harridge, Ralph W. Cannon '27, James Crusinberry '08, James T. Gallagher '33, William P. Hayes '20, Harold Johnson '10, Marvin W. McCarthy '30, Harry McNamara '24, Steward Owen '32, Oscar Reichow '10, Thomas Siler '39.

Cincinnati: Bob Newhall '19, Charles O'Connor '11, Frank W. Rostock '09, Bob Saxton '37.

Cleveland: Stuart M. Bell '20, William G. Evans '23, Howard Preston '39, Dan Taylor '22, Eugene J. Whitney '32, Thomas L. Terrell '10, Alex Zirin '39.

Detroit: Malcolm Bingay, W. W. Edgar '24, Doc Holst '30, Charles A. Hughes '08, J. W. Kenney '39, H. A. Montgomery '22.

New York: John A. Hydler, Ford C. Frick '23, Jose Aixala, Jr. '38, Christie Bohnsack '21, William E. Brandt '12, Edward T.

Brannick '36, George W. Daley '13, Stanley Frank '32, Earl H. Ferris '22, Nat Fleischer '11, Harry Forbes '37, Alan J. Gould '23, James M. Kahn '25, William Kane '32, John F. Keiran '22, George Kirksey '28, F. C. Lane '14, John Lardner '35, Frederick G. Lieb '11, Fred Linder, Stanley Lomax '26, Henry P. McLemore '35, William J. Manley '20, Arthur Mann '27, Tom Meany '24, Paul Mickelson '29, Arthur E. Patterson '39, Arthur Perrin '34, George E. Phair '19, Quentin Reynolds '31, Garry Schumacher '23, Jack Smith '36, Frank Wallace '26, Will Wedge '21, Wilbur Wood '13, Stanley Woodward '34, Richards Vidmer '22, Edward Zeltner '34.

Philadelphia: Joseph C. Dey '28, Bill Dooly '25, William Duncan '30, James Gantz '10, J. Herbert Good '32, Clair Hare '26, Al Horwits '26, Ross Kaufman '11, James F. Keirans '10, John I. Kolbmann '18, Joseph Labrum '22, Connie Mack, Robert T. Paul '25, Cy Peterman '23, Harry Robert '24, Stoney McLinn '08, Thomas D. Richter '10, Frank Ryan '25, A. E. P. Sensenderfer '18, Joseph Tumelty '27, William G. Weart '37.

Pittsburgh: Fred P. Alger '23, Claire M. Burcky '30, Dr. A. R. Cratty '09, D. E. Benjamin '28, Ray H. Gallivan '35, Richard Guy '09, George S. Jennings '24, James J. Long '09, James M. McAfee '16, James F. Murray '26, William P. Schragen '27, Carl Shatto '24, Fred S. Wertenbach '30, William A. White '17.

St. Louis: Cullen Cain '21, George Henger '16, Damon Kerby '27, Clarence F. Lloyd '10, San Muchnick '26, Leighton Rutledge '29, Maurice O. Shevlin '30, J. G. Taylor Spink '12.

Washington: H. C. Byrd '16, Kirk Miller '23, Frank F. O'Neill '11, Denman Thompson '15, Frank H. Young '22.

Gus Falzer, *Newark, N. J.;* Joseph McGlone, *Providence, R. I.;* Al Lang, *St. Petersburg, Florida.*

Index

Williams, Joe, 105
Williams, Ted, 100
Wilson, Hack, 144
Wilson, Jimmy, 3
Woodling, Gene, 148, 150, 154
Worcester, N. Y., 15, 43-44, 48, 157

World Series, *1929*, 142-44
  1950, 141, 145-56
Wright, Ed, 102
Wynn, Early, 63
Wyrostek, Johnny, 123

Youngman, Henny, 72
Yvars, Sal, 76